STUDIES IN RELIGIOUS POETRY
OF THE
SEVENTEENTH CENTURY

BY THE SAME AUTHOR

John Wesley in Lincolnshire
John Wesley: His Conferences and His Preachers
Published by The Epworth Press

STUDIES IN RELIGIOUS POETRY *of the* SEVENTEENTH CENTURY

By
W. L. DOUGHTY, B.A., B.D.

WIPF & STOCK · Eugene, Oregon

Wipf and Stock Publishers
199 W 8th Ave, Suite 3
Eugene, OR 97401

Studies in Religious Poetry of the Seventeenth Century
By Doughty, W. L.
Copyright©1946 Methodist Publishing - Epworth Press
ISBN 13: 978-1-5326-3515-1
Publication date 5/3/2017
Previously published by Epworth Press, 1946

Every effort has been made to trace the current copyright
owner of this publication but without success. If you have
any information or interest in the copyright,
please contact the publishers.

TO

MY DAUGHTERS

PHYLLIS ANNE

AND

JUDITH HELEN LAMPLOUGH

FOR THE JOY THEY GIVE ME AND THE HOPES THEY INSPIRE

Dreams, books, are each a world; and books, we know,
Are a substantial world, both pure and good:
Round these, with tendrils strong as flesh and blood,
Our pastime and our happiness will grow.

WORDSWORTH: *Personal Talk*

Contents

PREFACE	ix
1. RELIGION UNDER THE STARS Henry Vaughan—1622–95.	1
2. A MYSTIC IN HALF-LIGHTS Francis Quarles—1592–1644.	15
3. CROSS AND CRUCIFIX Richard Crashaw—*circa* 1612–49	34
4. THE SCRUTINY OF THE SOUL Sir John Davies—1569–1626.	60
5. A CYNIC AMONG SECTARIES Henry More—1614–87.	100
6. SONGS OF SPIRITUAL 'FELICITIE' Thomas Traherne—*circa* 1636–74.	150
NOTES AND REFERENCES	183
APPENDIX	194
INDEX	195

Preface

THIS IS NOT a book of literary criticism, but of personal predilections. The cynic may remark that this is merely another name for the same thing, which is not strictly true. With style, prosody, verse forms, there is little concern in these pages; not because these matters are without interest or importance, but because three hundred years have passed since each finger wrote,

> *nor all thy Piety nor Wit*
> *Shall lure it back to cancel half a Line,*
> *Nor all thy Tears wash out a Word of it.*

What the fingers have written they have written and there is little profit in discussing how these things might or should have been done, even if agreement were attainable.

In every case the quotations from the writings of the subjects of these studies are sufficient to enable the reader to form his own opinions on matters of style and to apply one of the soundest tests available to lovers of good literature: *Can I read this with a pleasure that is independent of the subject matter?* Whatever the answer may be, it is highly probable that it will incur the censure of Dr. A. or Professor B., but the reader need not be intimidated or discouraged on that account, for even those who occupy the magisterial seats in the Court of Literary Criticism are men—and women—whom common honesty would compel to confess: 'We also are men of like passions with you.'

Lest, however, in this matter of appreciation of literary style, the reader should be tempted to think more highly of himself than he ought to think, it is well to add the *caveat*: Take care that your taste be stimulated and cultivated by wide and selective reading and by a close acquaintance with the writings of those whom posterity has acclaimed masters of a great literary style.

Our concern is primarily with subject-matter. The general interest of these studies lies in the ways in which six men of intellectual vigour and undoubted piety looked at the perennial questions of religion, in an age whose mental climate was rapidly changing. The rigidity of the Scholastic Philosophy and its technique was being shaken, and men were proceeding to a closer examination of the phenomenal world in general, prior to advancing theories about it. Thinkers like Hobbes and Descartes were advocating a new approach to the ancient problems of philosophy and there were dim foreshadowings of modern scientific method. The intellectuals of this seventeenth century were poised between two mental worlds and their reactions are traceable in their writings. Some looked backward rather than forward: others, forward rather than backward; but in most cases there was a natural reluctance to commit themselves unreservedly to the general sweep of the intellectual current.

The names that will meet us here are not outstanding ones in the literature of the century; their owners were men of the by-ways, rather than the highways, and perhaps on that account more representative of the rank and file of those who read and thought on serious subjects. All were men of talent, taste, and education. Each study begins with a brief summary of the life of its subject and the position he held in society. Amongst them, Henry Vaughan and Richard Crashaw are best known to the general reader. Francis Quarles had, during and immediately after his lifetime, a great vogue in certain quarters which there is little prospect of his ever regaining. It was the common people who heard him gladly. I have more hope for the future of Sir John Davies, who, in my opinion, has never received the recognition that is his due. Henry More is of a different order. Beyond the others, his rugged, eccentric, heavily individualistic style, his queer and pedantic words and expressions, make against his ever becoming popular, even in select circles; but let the reader conquer these initial difficulties and he will be amply rewarded by the mordant satire, the subtle diagnoses of character, and the liberal opinions of a scholarly and devout soul. Thomas Traherne, whose brilliance was long eclipsed in the pages of a forgotten manuscript, is a recent star in the literary sky. His magnitude has not yet been assessed, but he already has his select public whose numbers will certainly increase.

Leisurely to follow trains of thought that an author starts is one of the joys of reading, and for many such a pleasant excursion we shall find ourselves indebted to these men. A few such journeyings are made in these studies, attempted in much the same spirit as a wanderer in some upland valley yields to the allurement of stepping stones over a stream; not because he wishes to gain the other bank—probably he does not—but just for the joy of going from stone to stone and thence returning. The pleasure is of the *going*, not of the journey's end. In the excursions here made the tracks sometimes wander rather far from their points of departure, but we need not be greatly concerned; always they come back to the highway they left.

To subject these men's religious beliefs, with their philosophical notions and implications, to such searching tests as modern knowledge and technique place at our disposal would not be difficult, but it would be ungracious and unprofitable. They were *seventeenth-* not twentieth-century men, and as such we must respect them. Their interest for us lies in part in the light which they shed upon the way in which rather ordinary, but educated people, both clerical and lay, looked at Religion, not only as a series of propositions for the acceptance of Faith, but also as a manner of life, in an age to which we to-day stand greatly indebted. Hence these studies are analytical and descriptive, rather than critical. I have tried to let the writers speak for themselves, venturing from time to time to interrupt their monologue, and the reader is invited to do the same.

The occasional references to John and Charles Wesley arise from a long and close interest in these remarkable men. They inevitably invite comparison with their predecessors of the previous century who were of similar mettle and cherished, as they did, what Henry Scougal felicitously called *The Life of God in the Soul of Man*.

Readers should note that the spelling in the quotations has been very carefully checked and any deviation from the authority of *The Oxford Dictionary* is merely the archaic spelling of the original text.

Those unacquainted with *The Testament of Beauty* of Robert Bridges should know that the poet had his own system of spelling and punctuation and never commenced his lines with a capital letter unless the initial word was a proper noun or followed a full-stop.

I am very grateful to my friend, Mr. John Purcell, of Redditch, for reading through the proofs; and also to my Wife and 'the Family'.

I also wish to record my deep appreciation of the consideration and courtesy of the Rev. Edgar C. Barton, of The Epworth Press.

The small figures in the text indicate notes and references at the end of the book. For certain abbreviations and editions used see I. 13 and II. 1.

W. L. D.

REDDITCH, WORCS.
March, 1946.

Acknowledgements

I WISH TO express my gratitude to the authors, or their representatives, and to the publishers for permission to quote from the following works:

The Destiny of Man by Nicolas Berdyaev. Published by Geoffrey Bles.

Poems of Rupert Brooke. Published by Sidgwick and Jackson.

The Testament of Beauty, by Robert Bridges. Published by the Clarendon Press.

Collected Poems of Walter de la Mare. Published by Faber and Faber.

Tragedy, by Professor W. Macneile Dixon. Published by Edward Arnold & Co.

Poems, by T. Sturge Moore. Published by Macmillan & Co.

Verse Translations of Greek Plays, by Sir Gilbert Murray. Published by George Allen and Unwin.

Saint Joan, by G. Bernard Shaw. Published by Constable & Co.

The Elizabethan World Picture, by Dr. E. M. W. Tillyard. Published by Chatto and Windus.

Adventures of Ideas, by Professor A. N. Whitehead. Published by the Cambridge Press.

The Seventeenth Century Background, by Professor Basil Willey, King Edward VII Professor of English Literature in the University of Cambridge. Published by Chatto and Windus.

I am especially indebted to Messrs. Percy J. and Arthur E. Dobell of Tunbridge Wells for their generous permission to quote extensively from the *Poems of Thomas Traherne*, of which they hold the copyright.

My thanks are also due to the Epworth Press for permission to incorporate an article contributed to *The London Quarterly and Holborn Review* for October, 1942, on Henry Vaughan, in the study entitled 'Religion under the Stars.'

W. L. D.

I

Religion under the Stars

Henry Vaughan—1622–95

NESTLING shyly amongst the hymns on 'Love and Communion' in the Methodist Hymn-book is one which begins: 'My soul, there is a country,' ascribed to a certain Henry Vaughan. Neither its music nor its phraseology is of our time, and in some religious atmospheres it would be highly incongruous. There is about it the fragrance of other days, when men thought spiritually in terms of pictures rather than of metaphysics, and were prepared to break a lance with those who claimed the ministries of Beauty and Poetry for mundane and temporal things alone.

As the later Elizabethans passed away, earthly love became increasingly the theme of English poetry; some of it delicate and tender; some striving after quaint and extravagant conceits; some sensual and unsavoury. Toward the end of the year 1610 a young Cambridge undergraduate whose name was George Herbert wrote to his mother bewailing 'the vanity of these many love-poems, that are daily writ and consecrated to Venus', and 'that so few are writ, that look toward God and Heaven'. With his letter he enclosed a sonnet:

> *My God, where is that ancient heat towards thee,*
>   *Wherewith whole showls of Martyrs once did burn,*
>   *Besides their other flames? Doth Poetry*
> *Wear Venus Livery? only serve her turn?*

> *Why are not* Sonnets *made of thee? and layes*
>   *Upon thine Altar burnt? Cannot thy love*
>   *Heighten a spirit to sound out thy praise*
> *As well as any she? Cannot thy* Dove
> *Outstrip their* Cupid *easily in flight?*
>   *Or, since thy ways are deep, and still the same,*
>   *Will not a verse run smooth that bears thy name!*[1]

Herbert himself was amongst the earliest of those whose spirit the love of God first 'heightened' thus to sound out His praise, and when he died at forty years of age the English Muse was still shy of these unwonted themes. Soon, however, she gathered strength and courage, and Religion had her 'nest of singing birds'. Amongst the songsters was Henry Vaughan. He was born in or about 1622 at Newton St. Bridget on the Usk. After Oxford and a spell in London, where he studied law and met many leading literary men of the day at the 'Globe' Tavern, he qualified in medicine and returned to his native and beloved Usk country, practised there, and died in 1695. There is little else to record. Some time before 1650 sickness endangered his life and even as late as 1654 he considered himself 'at no great distance from death'. It was at this time that he came under the posthumous influence of 'the blessed man, Mr. George Herbert', and underwent a spiritual conversion. Herbert had died in 1633. Influenced, doubtless, by his friends of the 'Globe' Tavern, Vaughan had become a writer of verse, and had boasted of his gay life in Town, probably exaggerating its profligacy in the interests of a youthful desire to be regarded as one of the fashionable rakes of the day. Now all was changed. Just as his more distinguished predecessor, John Donne (Vaughan was born in 1622 and Donne died in 1631), regretted the poetry of his youth and devoted his pen to the service of God and religion, so Vaughan renounced his earlier work and begged 'most humbly and earnestly' that it might not be read. Henceforward he became a 'dedicated spirit'.

That Vaughan derived some of his inspiration from George Herbert is beyond doubt; indirectly he confesses it. In many of his passages we can hear the parson of Bemerton speaking again, and those who are edified by taking note of plagiarisms and imitations can easily compile their own lists or accept those of the pundits who delight in this kind of work. It is, however, of far greater consequence to know that Vaughan was no mere vulgar plagiarist.[2] Taken as a whole, his religious poetry has never had the wide appeal of Herbert's, but in his greatest moments he rises to heights of beauty that his predecessor never reached. Herbert is always the parish priest and successor of Chaucer's 'persoun', for

> *Cristes lore and his apostles twelve,*
> *He taughte, and first he folwed it himselve.*[3]

His verse reveals how his life revolved about ecclesiastical customs and buildings; doctrines and creeds; festivals and saints' days; and one sees him in Bemerton Church, as Walton has pictured him, 'left there alone to toll the bell', or 'lying prostrate on the ground before the altar.' The titles of his poems alone are a miniature compendium of religious and ecclesiastical themes. He is, however, a very lovable parish priest, of the type whose fragrance still lingers here and there in the Anglican Church.

Vaughan, in contrast, is not the priest, nor yet that oddity, the ecclesiastically-minded layman. His love for the English Church is, none the less, deep and true, and he mourns the cleavages which have occurred in his time. Herbert views the English Church and compares it with that of Rome, with contented and slightly unctuous thankfulness:

> *Blessed be God, whose love it was*
> *To double-moat thee with His grace,*
> And none but thee,

he sings. In Vaughan's poem with the same title, *The*

British Church, there is the note of alarm and distress and he prays for Divine intervention:

> *Haste, haste, my dear!*
> *The souldiers here*
> *Cast in their lots again,*
> *That seamless coat,*
> *The Jewes touch'd not,*
> *These dare divide and stain.*

Vaughan's thought has a more distant horizon. A section of the Church, specially blessed by God and 'double-moated with His grace' hardly accords with a conception of the Church Universal, in which every schism is a wrong done to the Body of Christ.

That freer, wider outlook prevails in his verse. Though Vaughan was no ecclesiastic, his religious ideas are scrupulously correct. As one would expect, some of his phraseology is apt to embarrass those who, whilst holding in the main his doctrines, cannot entirely clothe them in his verbal forms. Apparently he found that orthodoxy supplied his needs and its current phraseology expressed his thought, for he ventured on no flight of theological speculation on his own account. Therein lies much of his charm. It is the charm of a *naïveté* of expression such as characterizes some Methodist hymns, and he who reads aright feels the more surely the pulsations of the heart of truth because of the sweet whimsicality of the body through which its tides flow. Vaughan believed that a man's salvation results from his assent to certain revealed truths, and these he himself apparently accepted without intellectual difficulty or mental reservation. In his verses there is no suggestion that

> *He fought his doubts and gathered strength,*
> *He would not make his judgment blind,*
> *He faced the spectres of the mind*
> *And laid them,*[4]

which is one reason why to read them is to add to life's

tranquillity. It is good sometimes to escape from both the prose and verse of religious controversy. If he had his 'doubts' and 'spectres', he did not sing about them. When a man makes such subjects the themes of his song it is tempting to wonder whether they are objects of æsthetic interest to him rather than sinister potentials that threaten the foundations of his spiritual life and peace of mind. Briefly, it may be said of Vaughan that he writes much of the '*bloud*' of Christ, and a vicarious and sacrificial doctrine of the Atonement was the basis of all his hopes.

Throughout his work there breathes a deep sense of sin, and his language of contrition and self-condemnation is as severe as any to be found in the literature of human penitence.

> *In all this* Round *of life and death*
> *Nothing's more vile than is my breath:*
> *Profaneness on my tongue doth rest,*
> *Defects and darkness in my brest:*
> *Pollutions all my body wed,*
> *And even my soul to thee is dead,*[5]

is but one sample, and one pauses to question the entire sincerity of such sentiments. It can only be a superficial sincerity for the last statement is obviously untrue. A soul wholly dead to God could never entertain such thoughts of its own corruption nor thus face its own inwardness; but it is easy to exaggerate when contemplating one's own emotions and so to indulge in a luxurious kind of grief. The question is raised whether verse is a possible medium for the expression of a sense of exceeding great and bitter sinfulness. Does a man with such a consciousness of sin want to express it at all: less still become lyrical about it, unless for the time being he has vacated the *rôle* of sinner for that of psychologist? Such is, apparently, a transition which some find it easy to effect, and then a man's sin is no longer something stark, unyielding, demonic, against which he raves and batters himself in vain, but rather a prepared laboratory piece, washed clean of dust and tears and blood; holding slender connexion with its crude, formless prototype, and liable to 'melt into air, into thin air', as if it were 'such stuff as dreams are made on', which is probably what in the main it is. It may be objected that Cowper, labouring under a deep sense of sin and convinced that forgiveness was impossible, poured out his tortured soul in verse:

> *Damned below Judas; more abhorred than he was,*
> *Who for a few pence sold his holy Master!*
> *Twice-betrayed Jesus me, the last delinquent,*
>   *Deems the profanest.*

We know these words to be utterly sincere, and they are strong language; but the verses are headed: *Lines written under the Influence of Delirium.* Cowper was insane when he wrote them, and the verse of sane men is our concern.

Where the sense of sin finds true poetic expression it is surely sin, not in its solitary, menacing nakedness and crudity, and present actuality, but sin now forgiven and no longer formidable, powerful and wholly dominant: sin whose power is broken and whose sting is taken away. Between a poet like Vaughan and this sin of his there stands the Cross of Christ. 'See, see', shrieks Kit Marlowe's Faust,

> *where Christ's blood streams in the firmament!*
> *One drop would save my soul, half a drop! ah, my Christ!;*[6]

but Faust was on the farther side of that streaming blood; for Vaughan it came between him and his sin, and the difference is that between Hell and Heaven. There is, insists Vaughan, no deliverance save through Him 'whose blood peace brings';[7] who

> *by His blood did us advance*
> *Unto His own Inheritance.*[8]

Therefore,
> *O hear, my God! hear Him, whose bloud*
> *Speaks more and better for my good!*[9]

So he calls not only on man, but, with St. Paul's feeling for the wider creation, on 'trees, flowers, and herbs; birds, beasts, and stones',

> *Lift up your heads and leave your moans!*
> *For here comes he*
> *Whose death will be*
> *Man's life, and your full liberty.*[10]

That conception of 'the whole creation groaning and travailing in pain', with the hope of its being one day 'delivered from the bondage of corruption into the liberty of the glory of the children of God'[11] has never ceased to haunt the minds of Christian thinkers, and it has gained renewed vitality from the pressure of events today. Elsewhere, as he sings out his plea for his own deliverance, the note of passion steals into his verse:

> *open to*
> *A sinful wretch, a wretch that caus'd thy woe:*
> *Thy woe, who caus'd his weal: so far his weal*
> *That thou forgott'st thine own, for thou didst seal*
> *Mine with thy blood, thy blood which makes thee mine,*
> Mine ever, ever: and me ever thine.[12]

It is, then, out of sin remembered but forgiven, rather than continuing and unforgiven, that Vaughan's songs arise. Of greater verses than his it is true that they are great because, not sin, but salvation, is their real theme. No man can be lyrical about sin unless he is first lyrical about salvation. There lies part, at any rate, of the secret of those hymns of Charles Wesley which, in the *Hymn-book* of 1779, appear in the section 'For Mourners convinced of Sin'. Sin is never seen in its true colours till men are *convinced* that it *is* sin; and there could be no such conviction nor could those hymns ever have been written if there had not been in the writer's mind far more than a glimmer of understanding of the theme of a later section, 'For Believers Saved'. A man must at least have some appreciation of the meaning of

> *Mercy for all who know not God;*
> *Mercy for all in Jesus's blood;*
> *Mercy that earth and heaven transcends;*
> *Love that o'erwhelms the saints in light;*
> *The length, and breadth, and depth, and height*
> *Of love divine, which never ends,*[13]

and a deep desire for the experience, before he can sing

> *Wretched, helpless, and distrest,*
> *Ah, whither shall I fly?*
> *Ever gasping after rest,*
> *I cannot find it nigh:*
> *Naked, sick, and poor, and blind,*
> *Fast bound in sin and misery. . . .*

and even then the vital experience creeps in and the real time sequence is revealed, for the verse finishes with the plea,

> *Friend of sinners, let me find*
> *My help, my all in thee.*[14]

No man can sing greatly of sin who has not seen above and beyond it the forgiving, redeeming love of God. So Vaughan, like many another who has known its blighting power—'Is there any murth'rer worse than sin?'[15] he asks—achieves, through faith in Christ's 'bloud,' his soul's release.

The Christian life is, however, one of struggle, and no man dares to say of any battle of his spirit that it is the last. Hence not all Vaughan's verse breathes 'the peace and joy of faith'. Again and again he deplores his inconstancy and temporary estrangement from God, and his prayers for forgiveness and renewal shape themselves in beauty.

> *Open my rockie heart, and fill*
> *It with obedience to thy will:*
> *Then seal it up, that as none see,*
> *So none may enter there but Thee.*[16]

> *Touch with one coal*
> *My frozen heart!* *And with thy secret key*
> *Open my desolate rooms...*[17]

Here is the prayer of a man who believes his own life's possibilities to be far greater than its achievements and needing only the alchemy of Divine grace to set them free; and lest that belief should engender aught of pride; or the distractions of activity, however beneficent, destroy life's calm, he prays also,

> *Give me humility and peace.*[18]

He had an unerring instinct for the treasures that neither moth nor rust can corrupt and that thieves cannot break through nor steal.

Vaughan, then, mystic that he is, sings glad-hearted of God's direct action upon his soul, and the grace mediated through Jesus Christ. There is, however, a grace of God that reaches men through earthly things and those who have the double grace find a double blessedness in life. Francis Thompson knew how true that is and in his essay on *Nature's Immortality* declared it in music of word and thought:

Absolute Nature lives not in our life, nor yet is lifeless, but lives in the life of God: and in so far, and so far merely, as man himself lives in that life, does he come into sympathy with Nature, and Nature with him. She is God's daughter, who stretches her hand only to her Father's friends.

There is profound religious truth in Coleridge's line:

> *Therefore all seasons shall be sweet to thee.*[19]

They were sweet to Vaughan, and with their sweetness, that of Nature, his songs are fragrant. Dr. Edwyn Bevan tells how one day, in the Ashmolean Museum at Oxford, he was looking through Turner's water-colours of that city, and 'when I went out again . . . into the Oxford streets, it all looked different; there were new lights on trees and houses; it all looked like a painted picture by Turner'.[20] Even so the beauty of the world is different to him who has seen the beauty of God in Christ Jesus: that is, if he regards the beauty of the world at all.

> *My world this day has lovely been—*
> *But not like what the child has seen,*[21]

sang W. H. Davies. To any Nature-lover the world is lovely, but to the child of God to whom has come the grace that is in Christ Jesus, a more subtle beauty is revealed, and all the loveliness of *things* is a further revelation of the loveliness of *God*.

That is how Henry Vaughan saw Nature, and to one aspect of it he returns again and again: to night and the stars, whose 'fair, ordered lights'[22] shine again and again in his verse. His was a spirit kindred to that of the writer of the Eighth Psalm. Few people in Vaughan's day could have beheld, more frequently than he,

> *upon the night's starr'd face*
> *Huge cloudy symbols of a high romance,*[23]

for was he not a country doctor! 'High romance' was indeed there for him because God was there, stirring 'immortal longings' in him; those longings which have united generations of watching, wondering men in a common emotional experience. Few are the poets whose thoughts keep company with those of Sir Henry Wotton:

> *You meaner Beauties of the Night,*
> *That poorly satisfy our Eyes*
> *More by your number, than your light,*
> *You Common-people of the Skies;*
>   *What are you when the Sun shall rise?*[24]

Writing in his *Journal* on 17th April 1855, Amiel expressed what the finest and most reverent souls have ever felt:

The weather is still incredibly brilliant, warm and clear. The day is full of the singing of birds, the night is full of stars. . . . Nature has become all kindness, and it is a kindness clothed upon with splendour.

For nearly two hours have I been lost in the contemplation of this magnificent spectacle. I felt myself in the temple of the infinite, in the presence of the worlds, God's guest in this vast nature. The stars wandering in the pale ether drew me far away from earth. What peace beyond the power of words, what dews of life eternal, they shed on the adoring soul! I felt the earth floating like a boat in this blue ocean. Such deep and tranquil delight nourishes the whole man . . . it purifies and ennobles. I surrendered myself, . . . I was all gratitude and docility.

Four days later—this!

I felt the unfathomable thought of which the Universe is the symbol live and burn within me; I touched, proved, tasted, embraced my nothingness and my immensity; I kissed the hem of the garments of God, and gave Him thanks for being Spirit and for being Life. Such moments are glimpses of the divine.

Vaughan had those moments. On horse-back and solitary beneath the stars many of his verses must have come to him and the night wind have been as the breath of God. He writes on *Midnight*:

> *When to my eyes,*
>   *Whilst deep sleep others catches,*
>   *Thine host of spyes,*
> *The Starres, shine in their watches,*
>   *I doe survey*
>   *Each busie ray,*
> *And how they work and wind,*
>   *And wish each beame*
>   *My soul doth streame*
> *With the like ardour shin'd.*

Picture him again, out on a night of

windy weather,
Clouds and blown stars and broken light;[25]

envying the people who are at home and in bed, and yet

grateful for all journeying mercies—more to him than to most men! Listen to him!

> Stars are of mighty use. *The night*
> *Is dark, and long:*
> *The Rode foul: and where one goes right,*
> *Six may go wrong.*
> *One twinkling ray,*
> *Shot o'er some cloud,*
> *May clear much way,*
> *And guide a croud.*[26]

Thus the natural man, with his little grumble and his flickering hope! But, as he writes elsewhere, 'all things here show him heaven'; so,

> *God's Saints are shining lights: who stays*
> *Here long must passe*
> *O're* [sic] *dark hills, swift streames, and steep ways*
> *As smooth as glasse:*
> *But these all night,*
> *Like Candles, shed*
> *Their beams, and light*
> *Us into Bed.*
> *They are indeed our Pillar-fires,*
> *Seen as we go:*
> *They are that Citie's shining spires*
> *We travell to.*[27]

Thus he knew, like one of long ago, 'the night shall be light about me; even the darkness hideth not from Thee.'[28]

In one of his poems, *The Night*, he recalls lovingly how, in this the season of his own closest approach and sweetest communion, Nicodemus came to Jesus and

> *saw such light*
> *As made him know his God by night.*

More and more this becomes his 'hour of knowing':

> *Dear night! this world's defeat:*
> *The stop to busie fools: care's check and curb:*
> *The day of spirits: my soul's calm retreat*
> > *Which none disturb.*

It is also 'God's knocking time', that God in whom

> *There is ... some say,*
> *A deep, but dazzling darkness; as men here*
> *Say it is late and dusky, because they*
> > *See not all clear.*
> *O for that night! where I in him*
> *Might live invisible and dim!*

As a country doctor and a man of sincere piety, not only did the darkness become light about him, but he could say,

> *Death met I too,*
> *And saw the dawn glow through,*[29]

and in that dawn he saw again the faces of his own loved ones who had gone into 'the world of light'. His songs proclaim how, as life's experiences crowded in upon him, death and darkness held less and less dominion over him, and he sings:

> *Dear, beauteous death; the Jewel of the Just!*
> *Shining no where but in the dark;*
> *What mysteries do lie beyond thy dust,*
> > *Could man outlook that mark!*
>
> *He that hath found some fledg'd bird's nest may know*
> > *At first sight if the bird be flown;*
> *But what fair dell or grove he sings in now,*
> > *That is to him unknown.*
>
> *And yet, as Angels in some brighter dreams*
> > *Call to the soul when man doth sleep,*
> *So some strange thoughts transcend our wonted theams,*
> > *And into glory peep.*[30]

Under his beloved night sky we leave him. His 'peep' into 'glory' has become a song in his heart. Stars and stars and stars! Yes—but beyond the stars!—What? Being a poet he does not weigh the niceties of Copernican astronomy, beginning then to exercise the minds and revolutionize the thinking of men—we will forgive him that—but sings out in glorious confidence his faith, his hope, his prayer:

> *My Soul, there is a countrie*
>   *Afar beyond the stars,*
> *Where stands a winged Sentrie*
>   *All skilfull in the wars.*
>
> .   .   .   .   .
>
> *If thou canst get but thither,*
>   *There growes the flowre of peace,*
> *The rose that cannot wither,*
>   *Thy fortresse and thy ease.*
> *Leave then thy foolish ranges;*
>   *For none can thee secure,*
> *But One, who never changes,*
>   *Thy God, thy Life, thy Cure.*[31]

There, in high, imaginative moments he loves to dwell,

> *Where no rude shade, or night*
> *Shall dare approach us; we shall there no more*
>   *Watch stars, or pore*
>   *Through melancholy clouds, and say*
>   *Would it were day!*
> *One everlasting* Saboth *there shall runne*
> *Without* Succession, *and without a* Sunne.[32]

II

A Mystic in Half-lights

Francis Quarles—1592–1644

IT IS A tribute to Francis Quarles that in almost every anthology of English poetry he is represented, and he contributes one beautiful little lyric to the *Methodist Hymnbook*. That distinction alone should entitle him to remembrance. In his own day he was highly esteemed in the more Puritanical coteries of society; so much so that at one period the absurd notion was put abroad that Milton was directly in his debt. We have confirmation of this from no less a person than John Wesley. William Law had suggested that Isaac Newton had derived his three laws of Matter and Motion from the eccentric mystic, Jacob Behmen; that: 'Sir Isaac Newton ploughed with Jacob Behmen's heifer.' In a letter to Law dated 6th January 1756, Wesley curtly dismisses this suggestion with the words: 'Just as much as Milton ploughed with Francis Quarles's heifer.'[1]

Literary fashions change, and in the course of years once-popular names become known only to the few. Such is the fate of Quarles. He was born near Romford, Essex, in 1592, in the manor house of Stewards, his father's home. After education at Cambridge and Lincoln's Inn, he went to Heidelberg in the train of the Princess Elizabeth, daughter of King James the First, when, in 1613, she married Frederick, the Elector Palatine. Later he lived in Ireland as secretary to Archbishop Ussher of Armagh, and in 1639 he was appointed chronologer to the City of London, a post which he held until his death.

His political sympathies during those disturbed times were with King Charles the First, whom he visited at Oxford early in 1644. In consequence, his property was sequestrated, his manuscripts burnt, and a petition to Parliament preferred against him. In his wife's words, 'this struck him so to the heart that he never recovered it.' In September 1644 he died.

From about the year 1620 he was continuously engaged in literary work, chiefly in verse and dealing mainly with moral and religious themes. It is almost exclusively upon one volume, *Emblems*, that his claim to recognition rests and with that alone we are now concerned. The 'emblems' in question are of two kinds: poems, of which there are fifteen in each of five books, and allegorical pictures, one to illustrate each poem. These latter are quaint, often droll productions, and are an interesting study in themselves.

Quarles tells us on the first page why he wrote his book.

> *Reader, this book shall teach the pious heart*
> *To soar from earth, and better views impart:*
> *Flaming with zeal to rise to Heaven above,*
> *And make the Triune God the object of its Love.*

Whether he goes the best way to achieve his object is a very open question. His verse in general is smooth and easy and can be read with pleasure, especially as the poems are composed in varied metres. He has a good ear and rarely descends to doggerel, nor is there any sense of strain in his composition, however far-fetched his similes and metaphors may be. He uses words and expressions which are more uncouth and grating to modern ears than they would be to those of his own age. To address one's audience, even though unseen, as

> *Dunghill worldlings, you that root like swine,*[2]

may be symbolically correct, but it is not exactly a tactful or conciliatory line of approach: whilst

> *The way's not easy where the prize is great:*
> *I hope no virtues, where I smell no sweat,*[3]

may be shrewd, but is scarcely elegant.

On one occasion he appears to divide his fellow mortals into three classes, in a couplet worthy of the genius of Alexander Pope in one of his most mordant moods:

> *We'll look to Heaven, and trust to higher joys;*
> *Let swine love husks, and children whine for toys*[4]

—though Pope, we may be sure, would have reversed the order of the lines.

At times his infelicities border upon irreverence, though such a suggestion would have shocked him deeply.

> *Thy Godhead, Jesus, are the flames that fry me,*[5]

and

> *Thou [God] art the treacle that must make me sound,*[6]

are examples. In like mood he exclaims,

> *My marrow melts, my fainting spirits fry*
> *In the torrid zone of thy meridian eye:*[7]

sentiments which even the oil of alliteration cannot render smooth and palatable to a fastidious literary taste or reconcile to a reverent mind. In reference to the Person of Christ he suggests that

> *the human nature*
> *Is made the umbrella to the Deity:*[8]

a conception which does not appear to have occurred to the reverend Fathers who gathered at Nicæa and Constantinople.

As we have seen, he uses alliteration freely, as when his

> *blustering Boreas blows the boiling tide;*[9]

a spirited performance which adds a touch of gaiety to an otherwise lugubrious address to Adam and Eve. One can only rejoice that metrical considerations precluded the use of 'billow' instead of 'tide'.

It were, however, greatly to be regretted should these

mannerisms and eccentricities deter any interested inquirer into the religious verse of this period from going farther. All poets have their moments of weakness, if not of bathos, and something must be allowed for the fashion of the times. Quarles regarded his ability to write in verse as a sacred gift and invoked Divine aid in its use. Nevertheless, he does not disdain the old classical mythology as a minor aid, but his use of it is very significant and obviously calculated. It is mainly satirical, and when dealing with human vices he frequently personifies them in the deities and sub-deities of Greece and Rome. They are, in fact, the demons of his drama, and thus Quarles alines himself with those Fathers of the Church to whom the gods of Paganism were emanations of evil, antagonistic to the true celestial hierarchy. In a similar manner, natural phenomena, when treated by Quarles apart from their divine significance or agency, are described in terms of the pagan myths. So we have the old, familiar paraphernalia; blustering Boreas, Circe's charms, Cupid's dart, Icarian wings, Danaë's showers, Stygian darkness, Sisyphean stones: after which we have every right to demand that Sol shall 'drive his chariot' and Prosper 'bring the day', which both obligingly do. Somehow or other it is not boring. These diaphanous figures lightly come and lightly go and we are spared the elaborations of the neo-classical school which was presently to arise.

Quarles is concerned to depict the woes that followed the Fall of Man, not as they afflicted our first parents, but as they were afflicting contemporary society. His poems start in Eden and the short dialogue between Eve and the Serpent is one of his most engaging ventures. Their talk lacks the Miltonic sweep and rhythm, but the words and style of Quarles's Serpent more aptly fit the occasion; they are realistic where those of Milton's are idealistic. The latter, after his preliminary flattery, reasons with a weight and eloquence which imply an Eve too sophisticated for an age of innocence, unless he was paying her a subtle compliment.

Indeed, if Eve's mind was of calibre sufficient to appreciate the measured arguments of Milton's Serpent, one may well doubt whether all the innate magic of the forbidden fruit was capable of sharpening its powers in any great degree. Quarles apparently knew the average woman better. His Eve is a less sophisticated being and more like the quite charming Eves that you and I will probably meet tomorrow. His Serpent asserts and coaxes, but argues little, whereas Milton's argues at length. How wise he was! Eve must be persuaded that God is mistaken in predicting that death will follow disobedience. It is to her senses rather than to her mind that he directs his appeal, and he woos her consent less by the validity of his logic than by the subtle intonations of his voice, by expatiating upon the alluring qualities and appearance of the fruit itself and by that personal flattery which is so often the final *argumentum ad feminam*. His honeyed words are skilfully chosen, arch, persuasive, making the desirable appear more desirable still:

> *Woman, do but taste:*
> *See how the laden boughs make silent suit*
> *To be enjoyed; look how their bending fruit*
> *Meet thee half-way: observe but how they crouch*
> *To kiss thy hand: coy woman, do but touch:*
> *Mark what a pure vermilion blush has dyed*
> *Their swelling cheeks, and how for shame they hide*
> *Their palsy heads, to see themselves stand by*
> *Neglected: woman, do but cast an eye.*

He is almost irresistible.

> *Stretch forth thy hand, and let thy fondness never*
> *Fear death: do, pull and eat, and live for ever.*
> EVE. *'Tis but an apple: and it is as good*
> *To do, as to desire. Fruit's made for food:*
> *I'll pull, and taste, and tempt my Adam, too,*
> *To know the secrets of this dainty.*
>
> SERPENT.   Do.[10]

The silky-toned voice has won and there is a touch of genius in the ending of the scene, the Serpent's seductive and triumphant *Do*. Thus encouraged and sustained Eve eats the apple, Adam follows her example, and Creation swings out into strange and sombre ways, for

That one hour did mar what Heaven six days was making.[11]

Hear Milton, however, on that same moment of Eve's fall, and the master poet stands revealed:

Earth felt the wound, and Nature from her seat
Sighing through all her works gave signs of woe,
That all was lost.[12]

Quarles now moves on to the world which human disobedience and folly have produced: a grim place, as seen through the poet's eyes. It was an age of tumult and ominous calm: of promise and frustration; an age which was trying desperately to adjust its confused affairs: in which political and religious antagonisms were bewilderingly mingled, and that was slipping fast and ever faster down the steep slope to civil war. His scorn of what he sees is unbounded and expressed in direct and superlative language. Yet he feels the pull of this fallen world upon himself, and through the whole series of poems we are aware of the tension in which his spirit was held. Vividly he sees

this dark fog
Of dungeon earth,[13]

and labours to express the vast, hideous horror of Evil, nor is he dainty in his choice of epithets; for a hideous thing he uses hideous words. That is wise. It is possible to write of Evil in terms so flamboyant as to make it almost attractive and thus to invest it with a spurious beauty that strengthens its appeal.

Presently, and quite surprisingly, Quarles introduces into his scheme the classical conception of a Golden Age: nothing less than the *Saturnia Regna* of Virgil, which

Tibullus describes so picturesquely. Saturn, Ruler of Olympus, having been overthrown and exiled by his son Jove, settled on the Capitoline Hill, built up an earthly kingdom on which he bestowed agricultural and other blessings, and later disappeared. It was reputed to be an age of simplicity, contentment, and peace, and Charles Wesley seems to have had it in mind when he wrote:

> *O, what an age of golden days!*[14]
>
> *Non acies, non ira fuit, non bella, nec ensem
> immiti saevus duxerat arte faber,*

and Quarles kindles to the warm admiration of the Roman poet with his

> *Quam bene Saturno vivebant rege!*[15]

But, since Eden's gates have closed, where in time can we place

> *this other Eden, demi-Paradise,
> This fortress built by Nature for herself
> Against infection and the hand of war,
> This happy breed of men, this little world?*[16]

The backward clanging of the gates ushered us into a world

> *degenerated, and become
> A base adulteress, whose false births do fill
> The earth with monsters—monsters that do roam
> And rage about, and make a trade to kill;*[17]

—Gluttony, Lechery, Pride, Avarice, Envy, Deceit and Sloth, the Seven Deadly Sins of medieval faith and fable, whose devastating power St. John of the Cross traces even in the soul of the Christian believer in his passage through 'the Dark Night of the Soul'.

Quarles does not solve our Golden Age problem, but goes on to declare that the gods of this second dynasty, the pantheon of Jove, are still alive in the vices, sufferings and follies of mankind.

> *Gone are those golden days, wherein*
> * Pale conscience started not at ugly sin:*
> *When good old Saturn's peaceful throne*
> * Was unusurped by his beardless son.*

With Saturn has gone Ops, his consort, the goddess of Plenty, and Astræa, the goddess of Justice, and their places have been taken by

> *froth-born Venus and her brat,*
> *With all that spurious brood young Jove begat.*

So

> *earth boiled with lust, with rage it burned,*
> *And ever since the world hath been*
> *Kept going with the scourge of lust and spleen.*[18]

It is an ugly picture, but it was there in the seventeenth century, as, in some degree, in every century, for him who had eyes to see; but he who sees little else is an unhappy wight indeed.

Around that unsavoury world Quarles's fascinated and somewhat morbid fancy plays. He dwells more upon what is earthy and sinful in man than upon what is heavenly and good. Perhaps he was of the company of those austere souls who find it easier to blame than to praise; assuredly he is more expansive on a gloomy than upon a happy theme. He tears the World's scanty raiment to tatters and exhibits it in all its naked horror and uncleanness. It is the Mammon of the New Testament: the gross and nauseating abortion of G. F. Watts's picture, 'royal, imperial, irresistible, and when all is said, *imbecile*'.[19] Having exposed its manifold indecencies he brands it as a liar:

> *False world, thou liest: thou canst not lend*
> * The least delight:*
> *Thy favours cannot gain a friend,*
> * They are so slight:*
> *Thy morning pleasures make an end*
> * To please at night:*

Poor are the wants that thou suppliest:
And yet thou vauntest, and yet thou vy'st
With heaven! fond earth, thou boastest; false world, thou liest....

Thy words are gold, but thy rewards
   Are painted clay.[20]

This is to him the night of the world, and in verses whose cadences are like echoes from the Prothalamium of some Elizabethan poet he sings:

> *Will't ne'er be morning? Will that promised light*
> *Ne'er break, and clear those clouds of night?*
>   *Sweet Phosphor, bring the day,*
>   *Whose conquering ray*
> *May chase these fogs: sweet Phosphor, bring the day.*[21]

Quarles has his foibles, some of which are those of an extreme Puritanism and often amusing to a later age. He looks, for example, upon all forms of sport with such disapproval as might have gained for him the headmastership of Kingswood School had he lived in Wesley's day.[22] After an acid description of a game of bowls and of the talk and actions of the players—

> *See how their curved bodies writhe, and screw*
> *Such antic shapes as Proteus never knew:*
> *One raps an oath, another deals a curse:*
> *He never better played: this never worse:—*

he likens life to a game of bowls, where

> *The world's the jack; the gamesters that contend*
> *Are Cupid, Mammon: that judicious friend,*
> *That gives the ground, is Satan: and the bowls*
> *Are sinful thoughts: the prize, a crown for fools.*
> *Who breathes that bowls not? What bold tongue can say,*
> *Without a blush, he hath not bowled today?*[23]

So now we know! That then recent discovery of Europe, Tobacco, also comes under the lash of his tongue:

> *Come, burst your spleens with laughter to behold*
> *A new-found vanity, which days of old*
> *Ne'er knew: a vanity that has beset*
> *The world, and made more slaves than Mahomet;*
> *That has condemned us to the servile yoke*
> *Of slavery, and made us slaves to smoke.*

Then it occurs to him, as he looks back on 'these days of old', that 'they were smoked and slaved as well as we', for

What's sweet-lipped Honour's blast but smoke? What's treasure But very smoke? And what more smoke than pleasure?[24]

So for a moment he stands in the company of the immortal Falstaff:

> *What is that word, honour? Air. A trim reckoning! . . .*
> *Therefore I'll none of it: honour is a mere scutcheon.*[25]

'But', pipes up a cynical voice from among the poet's auditors, 'did you not, in 1632, in order to increase your income, obtain a reversion on tobacco and tobacco pipes imported into Ireland?' Alas! and alas! It cannot be denied.

But

a foolish consistency is the hobgoblin of little minds, adored by little statesmen and philosophers and divines. . . . With consistency a great soul has simply nothing to do.[26]

Thus Emerson, in pontifical mood! On the principle, may we presume, that *plus ça change, plus c'est la même chose?*

The world then, as Quarles sees it, is a conglomeration of vanities and in his condemnation he is rigorous and peremptory. His is a type of mind which every age has known; that of those fearful souls who believe that their salvation lies more in being under law than under grace; censorious people, who build their own lives on a basis of prohibitions and would compel other people to do the same; who are happier with negatives than with positives, which they find rather bewildering; who feel it is safer to lie up in the straitened harbourage of the Ten Commandments than to cruise in the wide haven of St. Paul's Hymn to Love.[27]

We note that, whilst Quarles uses natural phenomena to illustrate his moral teaching, he is more impressed by Nature's utilitarian functions than by her æsthetic qualities. Take, for example, this expression of his regard for the earth:

> *I love (and have some cause to love) the earth:*
> * She is my Maker's creature, therefore good:*
> *She is my mother, for she gave me birth:*
>   She is my tender nurse: she gives me food.
>
> *I love the Air: her dainty sweets refresh*
> * My drooping soul, and to new sweets invite me:*
> *Her shrill-mouthed choir sustain me with their flesh,*
> * And with their Polyphonian notes delight me.*
>
> *I love the Sea, she is my fellow creature,*
> * My careful purveyor; she provides me store:*
> *She walls me round: she makes my diet greater:*
> * She wafts my treasure from a foreign shore.*[28]

Here we encounter that feeling for Nature which Dr. Syntax, for example, exhibited:

> *I will acknowledge that a goose*
> *Is a fine fowl of sovereign use:*
> *But for a picture she's not fitted—*
> *The bird was made but to be spitted.*
> *The pigeon, I'll be bound to show it,*
> *Is a fine subject for a poet;*
> *In the soft verse his mate he woos,*
> *Turns his gay neck, and bills and coos,*
> *And, as in amorous strut he moves,*
> *Soothes the fond heart of him who loves:*

> *But I'll not paint him, no, not I—*
> *I like him better in a pie,*
> *Well rubbed with salt and spicy dust,*
> *And thus embodied in a crust.*
>
> *A trout, with all its pretty dyes*
> *Of various hues, delights the eyes;*
> *Yet, I must own, that dainty fish*
> *Looks very handsome in a dish;*
> *And he must be a thankless sinner*
> *Who thinks a trout a paltry dinner.*[29]

It is to be hoped that as Quarles sat down before his game pie, with the echoes of those 'Polyphonian notes' ringing in his ears, he prefaced his repast in the same kindly and compassionate way as that friend of our childhood, the Walrus, as he gazed upon the unlucky oysters,

> *Holding his pocket handkerchief*
> *Before his streaming eyes.*[30]

It is a far cry from sentiments such as these to those of a certain Francis of Assisi, who said: 'I will go to preach unto my little sisters, the birds', and 'they did not depart until he had given them his blessing'; and further still to those of Him who said: 'Behold the birds of the heaven . . . your heavenly Father feedeth them.'[31]

To many people it must appear more than strange that a devout mind can feel no real tenderness for living and beautiful things nor quicken to a keen joy in their presence: and the more so when we remember that Quarles was a contemporary of that William Shakespeare who sang:

> *Under the greenwood tree*
> *Who loves to lie with me,*
> *And tune his merry note*
> *Unto the sweet bird's throat?*[32]

and much more of that ilk; and of Thomas Nashe, untimely dead, with his bird-note song:

> *Spring, the sweet Spring, is the year's pleasant king;*
> *Then blooms each thing, then maids dance in a ring,*
> *Cold doth not sting, the pretty birds do sing,*
> *Cuckoo, jug-jug, pu-we, to-witta-woo.*[33]

How one would welcome, in Quarles's verse, a touch of that tenderness of heart over living things that die, including birds, that John Donne shows!

> *He [Death] rounds the aire, and breaks the hymnique notes*
> *In birds (Heavens choristers,) organique throats,*
> *Which (if they did not dye) might seeme to bee*
> *A tenth ranke in the heavenly hierarchie.*[34]

Our absorptions and intensities tend to build a prison-house around us and to shut us out from a part of our rich heritage. By the very exclusiveness and concentration of his piety there were delicate nuances of beauty and truth in the world to which Quarles was blind and deaf. There would have been a happier strain in his verse if more frequently he had let

> *bright Titan dart his golden ray*
> *And with his riches glorify the day!*,

for then he almost approaches joviality, as

> *The jolly shepherd pipes, flowers freshly spring;*
> *The beasts grow gamesome, and the birds they sing:—*[35]

a bucolic rhapsody which lacks the rollicking abandon of Milton and sends us with keener relish to his heart-warming and engaging creatures, hilarious in Paradise, where

> *Sporting the lion ramped, and on his paw*
> *Dandled the kid; bears, tigers, ounces, pards,*
> *Gambolled before them; the unwieldy elephant*
> *To make them mirth used all his might, and wreathed*
> *His lithe proboscis.*[36]

Quarles sees man, with Eden behind him, stumbling forward, blind on a darkened road; a poor, helpless thing, with the marks of decay and death upon him, mistaking the blight for the bloom, the curse for the blessing. 'What's a man?' he asks. 'A proud inch of living earth.' Elsewhere,

> *A scuttle full of dust, a measured span*
> *Of flitting time: a furnished pack, whose wares*
> *Are sullen griefs and soul-tormenting cares:*
> *A vale of tears: a vessel tunned with breath,*
> *By sickness broached, to be drawn out by death.* [37]

However we may dislike or even resent such images of man, they do set forth a certain truth about him, but not by any means the whole truth. We turn with relief and a warm glow at the heart to a Hebrew writer of long ago on the same subject:

> *What is man, that Thou art mindful of him?*
> *And the son of man, that Thou visitest him?*
> *For Thou hast made him but little lower than God,*
> *And crownest him with glory and honour.* [38]

It is an annihilating pessimism that bids us accept the former view to the exclusion of the latter; a facile and dangerous optimism that does homage to the latter and rejects the former, and the harvest can only be the bitterness of shattered illusion. The wise man, knowing the needs of his heart, finds a place for both in his philosophy of life.

Devastating as Quarles's judgements upon the human scene are for the most part, he can, on occasion, feelingly express the heavenward view of our humanity, as in

> *My heart's a living temple, to entertain*
> *The King of Glory and His glorious train,*

and

> *My great Creator did inspire*
> *My chosen earth with that diviner fire*
> *Of reason; gave me judgement and a will:*
> *That, to know good: this, to choose good from ill;*

> *He put the reins of power in my free hand,*
> *And jurisdiction over sea and land:*
> *He gave me art to lengthen out the span*
> *Of life, and made me all in being man.*[39]

As the poems proceed there steals into them a deepening but transient note of joy, born of the reconciling love of God in Christ Jesus. It is not uniformly sustained. Then it is that we discover the mystic in him, 'a mystic in half-lights', for he never wholly escapes the darkening influence of a sinful world. There is very little eroticism in his writing, although toward the end of the book he draws freely upon the Canticles both for his imagery and his phraseology. If the sequence of the poems be any true guide, as it should be, the moments of union between his soul and God were very occasional. Quarles has no continuous enjoyment of the Divine favour. Never does he appear to reach that serene height where the soul sings:

> Now *I have found the ground wherein*
> Sure my soul's anchor may remain.[40]

His is a religion of ever-recurring contrition. He is ever seeking God, and even when he finds Him he re-commences his search under some other figure of speech. Like Christina Rossetti he could say:

> *Wearied of sinning,* wearied of repentance,
> *Wearied of self, I turn, my God, to Thee.*[41]

Of this vacillation he is acutely aware, as in this prayer for constancy:

> *Eternal God! O thou that only art*
>   *The sacred fountain of eternal light,*
> *And blessed lodestone of my better part,*
>   *O thou, my heart's desire, my soul's delight,*
> *Reflect upon my soul and touch my heart,*

> *And then my heart shall prize no good above thee;*
> *And then my soul shall know thee; knowing, love thee,*
> *And then my trembling thoughts shall never start*
> *From thy commands, or swerve the least degree,*
> *Or once presume to move, but as they move in thee.*[42]

There is no triumphant and abiding joy. Quarles's gladness is tepid and mostly of the subjunctive mood and a vague future tense. Rarely does he move to the lilting rhythm of a great ecstasy, nor does he thrill us, allure us and make us cry: 'This is what my soul desires and by God's enabling grace I will have it.' His desire to express the life of his spirit seems to wait upon his desire to write verse, and that, with rare exceptions, is fatal to true literary achievement. How markedly we see the reverse in Charles Wesley, for whom literary form and expression were merely the handmaids of an exultant joy in God that had to find an outlet! Quarles writes *about* a religious experience; Wesley writes *out of* one. Thus the former sings:

> *O groundless deeps! O love beyond degree!*
> *The offended dies to set the offender free.*[43]

The opening line raises expectations which the sequel fails to fulfil. We rise to fall. We are prepared to be moved, but there is no angel to stir the pool of our emotion. Hear now Charles Wesley as he similarly approaches his theme and mark how he continues it.

> *O unexampled love!*
>   *O all-redeeming grace!*
> *How swiftly didst thou move*
>   *To save a fallen race:*
> *What shall I do to make it known*
> *What thou for all mankind hast done?*[44]

The angel has descended and the waters have been moved at his coming.

Quarles's book reaches no illuminating or inspiring climax; unveils no apocalyptic splendour: no Mystic Rose of Dante; evokes no sounding of John Bunyan's trumpets from the battlements of the Unseen. His eyes were unobservant of so much of the beauty of his earthly way, that the things of heaven had to him a paler beauty. It was largely through this inability to behold what was crystal clear to some of his contemporaries, men like Herbert, Crashaw, Vaughan, and Traherne, that he failed to qualify for a high place among the Immortals. Taken out of its context, there is a sardonic note in the very last line of *Emblems*:

> *Heaven knows not what to make of what he made;*

but we may well believe that as his spirit passed *ex umbris et imaginibus in veritatem* his unclouded eyes discerned at last

> *a better path he missed, with fairer flowers.*[45]

We will take our farewell of Francis Quarles as we meet him in his happier moods and moments. Here is a part of one charming poem which he might fittingly have entitled *Mater Dolorosa*. In sorrowing tenderness and in a mood that is reminiscent of Constance in *King John*—

> *Grief fills the room up of my absent child,*
> *Lies in his bed, walks up and down with me*—[46]

the Virgin Mother (and surely she was one of Botticelli's piteous Madonnas of the sad eyes!) addresses her Babe, foreseeing, in her mother love, the harshness of His earthly way and the bitterness of the end thereof:

> *Ah! must these dainty little arms, that twine*
> *So fast about my neck, be pierced and torn*
> *With ragged nails? And must these brows resign*
> *Their crown of glory for a crown of thorn?*
> *Ah! must this blessed Infant taste the pain*
> *Of death's injurious pangs: nay, worse, be slain?*[47]

The centuries fade away and for a moment he stands emotionally with one of the greatest poets of the world's literary youth, Euripides. Listen to Medea saying farewell to her children before they go out to die:

> *Oh, darling hand! Oh, darling mouth, and eye,*
> *And royal mien, and bright brave faces clear,*
> *May you be blessed, but not here! . . .*
>   *Ah God, the glow*
> *Of cheek on cheek, the tender touch; and Oh,*
> *Sweet scent of childhood. . . . Go! Go! . . .*[48]

The pathos of life, Virgil's *sunt lachrymæ rerum*, is incident to every age and inspires the poetry of every generation.

The compilers of the current *Methodist Hymn-book* selected four stanzas of a much longer poem, and they are presented as a complete and charming lyric.

> *Thou art my life; if Thou but turn away,*
> *My life's a thousand deaths: Thou art my way!*
> *Without Thee, Lord, I travel not, but stray.*
>
> *My light Thou art; without Thy glorious sight*
> *My eyes are darkened with perpetual night:*
> *My God, Thou art my way, my life, my light.*
>
> *Thou art my way; I wander, if Thou fly:*
> *Thou art my light; if hid, how blind am I!*
> *Thou art my life; if Thou withdraw, I die.*
>
> *Disclose Thy sunbeams; close Thy wings and stay;*
> *See, see how I am blind, and dead, and stray,*
> *O Thou that art my light, my life, my way!*[49]

That a hymn-book is the right place for these verses admits of question.

Finally, take this stanza, not from the *Emblems*, but another work of his, *Divine Fancies*:

> *Close now thine eyes, and rest secure:*
> *Thy soul is safe enough: thy body sure;*
> *　He that loves thee, he that keeps*
> *And guards thee, never slumbers, never sleeps.*
> *The smiling conscience in a sleeping breast*
> *　Has only peace, has only rest:*
> *　The music and the mirth of kings*
> *Are all but very discords, when she sings:*
> *　Then close thine eyes and rest secure;*
> *No sleep so sweet as thine, no rest so sure.*

Alas! Quarles, and alas! Had your Muse been more faithful and consistent you might have been

> *Married to immortal verse*
> *Such as the meeting soul may pierce,*
> *In notes, with many a winding bout*
> *Of linked sweetness long drawn out.*[50]

III

Cross and Crucifix

Richard Crashaw—*circa* 1612–49

IN THE YEAR 1646 there was published in London a book of verse with the unusual feature of two title-pages: two separate volumes in one cover. The first was entitled *Steps to the Temple: Sacred Poems*, and the second *The Delights of the Muses, or Other Poems written on several Occasions*. Both were by 'Richard Crashaw, sometimes [*sic*] of Pembroke Hall and late fellow of S. Peter's Coll. in Cambridge'. A second edition appeared in 1648, 'wherein are added divers pieces not before extant'. Without this explanation the reader might be forgiven did he attribute the two books to separate authors. *Steps to the Temple* is indeed a book of 'Sacred Poems'; *Delights of the Muses*, whilst entirely virtuous, is not.

Richard Crashaw's life was marked by little incident apart from the disruption of its end. The son of a zealous and well-known Puritan divine, he was born *circa* 1612–15 and educated at Charterhouse and Pembroke Hall, Cambridge. In 1636 he went to Peterhouse, of which college he was elected a fellow the following year. From early days he was deeply devout and contemplated taking orders in the English Church. During his boyhood his father, whose piety was of a militant and anti-Roman order, died, and with the removal of his direct influence the son's mind acquired a strongly anti-Puritan bias. The growing strength of Puritanism, combined with its excesses and extravagances, and his personal contacts with Roman Catholics, unsettled his mind and modified his religious views, so that when the Civil War broke out and Peterhouse Chapel was sacked on 21st December 1643, by Parliamentarian troops, he declined, as a fellow, to sign the Solemn League and Covenant and was in consequence expelled. Thus ended the happiest period of his life.

After a short time in London and Oxford, he published his book, and in the same year, 1646, went to Paris, never to return to this country. There he was found in great poverty by an old friend and fellow poet, Abraham Cowley. By this time he had formally made his submission to the Roman Catholic Church. Cowley introduced him to Henrietta Maria, Queen of England, who was then in Paris and in whose honour Crashaw, stout royalist as he was, had already written several poems. The Queen sent him to Rome with an introduction to Cardinal Palotta, who employed him as a secretary. Crashaw's disgust and protest at what seemed to him the irreligious ways of the Cardinal's household led to unhappy and dangerous consequences, whereupon Palotta sent him to act as Canon of the Chapel of our Lady at Loretto, but on the way he was stricken by fever and died four months after arrival. His burial there was to Cowley the

> *most divine*
> *And richest offering of Loretto's shrine!*[1]

Such, in brief, is the story of a man who made no notable impact upon the life of his own time and who, apart from some Latin poems, left behind him only a slender volume of verse about whose quality critics failed to agree. Most intelligent readers hold today that the best of Crashaw's poetry will last as long as the English language endures or men are moved by the beauty of an exquisite line and a graceful fancy. The defects of his verse are patent to every reader, but the wise man does not read for these. We smile, or frown, at such astonishing *gaucheries* as

> *He's followed by two faithful fountains;*
> *Two walking baths, two weeping motions,*
> *Portable, and compendious oceans,*[2]

the reference being to the weeping eyes of Mary Magdalene as she attended our Lord; or the rhapsodizing of the Magi over the Infant Jesus:

> *Whose full and all-unwrinkled face*
> *Nor sinks nor swells with time or place;*
> *But every where, and every while*
> *Is one consistent, solid smile.*[3]

Such passages, however, with others that are flat or obscure, are less obtrusive today than once they were, for this is an age that does not expect perfection and which readily forgets the anguish of such infelicities for joy that some phrase or thought of rapturous beauty has been born into the world. So we read, in the same poem that contains the 'portable, and compendious oceans',

> *The dew no more will weep*
> *The primrose's pale cheek to deck:*
> *The dew no more will sleep*
> *Nuzzel'd in the lily's neck;*
> *Much rather would it be thy tear,*
> *And leave them both to tremble here,*

and straightway we forgive and forget. Such writing more than atones for 'the false wit, the glittering conceits and strained similes' which roused the ire of John Dryden and Alexander Pope, and leaves us grateful to Swinburne for his praise of 'the dazzling intricacy and affluence in refinements, the supple and cunning implication, the choiceness and subtlety of Crashaw'.[4]

Crashaw's themes are few, but, like the four strings of a

violin, capable of many melodies as the musician fingers them. He lives in the presence of the Cross, which, in all his thought, is never far away. It is to him an object of devotion as the very instrument of human redemption.

> *O sad, sweet Tree,*
> *Woeful and joyful we*
> *Both weep and sing in shade of thee.*[5]

Throughout his verse the weeping and the singing persist. The physical aspects of the Crucifixion exercise an almost morbid fascination over him. His is a type of piety, so natural to some and so alien to others, that finds satisfaction in the Adoration of the Cross or in a cult so modern as that of Devotion to the Sacred Heart of Jesus. His spiritual destiny is written in his verse. For such as he all roads lead to Rome. Puritan and Parliament, hustling him out of his Cambridge fellowship, only hastened the inevitable day when Crashaw would pack his bag and follow whither his questing spirit had led, to

> *the holy place wherein*
> *Sits the successor of the greatest Peter.*[6]

Edward Hutton's words are true: 'Crashaw could never have lived in the Establishment, at any rate as it then was; his was too sensuous, too passionate a religion for any but the most uncompromising master.'[7] The sequel is largely guess-work. Did he find, as other such pilgrims have done, the master whose rein checked the passion and outpouring of his free spirit? Could he say, with the Vicar of Bray,

> *The Church of Rome I found would suit*
> *Full well my constitution,*

or did he discover an interpretation of the familiar words of Juvenal which that cynical and close observer of his fellow men (and women) could not even have imagined:

> *Omnia Romæ*
> *Cum pretio?*[8]

Was a part of that price the muting of his music and the swift death that silenced it too soon?

> *Go, songs, for ended is our brief, sweet play;*
>   *Go, children of swift joy and tardy sorrow:*
> *And some are sung, and that was yesterday,*
> *And some unsung, and that may be tomorrow.*[9]

But for Crashaw there was no tomorrow. Death took him when he was but thirty-six, and how much would one give for those songs unsung, coloured, as inevitably they would have been, by experience wider than any that his cloistered life at Cambridge could give!

In thought we see him before the central symbol of his Faith, a Crucifix. His emotion finds expression in imagery reminiscent of Mark Antony's before the murdered body of Cæsar:

> *Had I as many eyes as thou hast wounds,*
> *Weeping as fast as they stream forth thy blood. . . .*
>
> *Over thy wounds now do I prophesy,—*
> *Which, like dumb mouths, do ope their ruby lips,*
> *To beg the voice and utterance of my tongue. . . .*[10]

To Crashaw the wounds of Jesus are both mouths and eyes:

> *O these wakeful wounds of Thine!*
>   *Are they mouths? or are they eyes?*
> *Be they mouths, or be they eyne,*
>   *Each bleeding part some one supplies.*
>
> *Lo! a mouth, whose full-bloom'd lips*
>   *At too dear a rate are roses:*
> *Lo! a blood-shot eye that weeps,*
>   *And many a cruel tear discloses.*[11]

Some of his language is even more strained and generally distasteful to the religious mind today:

> *Thee with Thyself they have too richly clad;*
>   *Opening the purple wardrobe in Thy side.*
> *O never could there be garment too good*
> *For Thee to wear, but this of Thine own blood.*[12]

The utter pity roused by the mangled body of the Crucified creates a passionate desire to share in His sufferings. Others, like the Mother of Jesus and Mary Magdalene, have shared in them; so also should he. Their tear-dimmed eyes fascinate and move him, as eyes always did. Such evidence of the grief of others was to him as Milton's 'soul of Orpheus', that could

>   *sing*
> *Such notes as, warbled to the string,*
> *Drew iron tears down Pluto's cheek,*[13]

Crashaw himself being *in loco Plutonis*. Others of his age stood before the Cross and mingled their tears with his. There was, for example, Phineas Fletcher (1582–1650) with his

> *Drop, drop, slow tears,*
>   *And bathe those beauteous feet*
> *Which brought from Heaven*
>   *The news and Prince of Peace:*
> *Cease not, wet eyes,*
>   *His mercy to entreat;*
> *To cry for vengeance*
>   *Sin doth never cease.*
> *In your deep floods*
>   *Drown all my faults and fears;*
> *Nor let His eye*
>   *See sin, but through my tears.*

There is no uniformity in the outgoings of the human spirit, and there were souls no less devout to whom the imagined sight of their Crucified Lord was so agonizing that they turned aside from it. Yet their insight into its meaning was equally searching and sincere. Of their number was John Donne. He has referred to 'Christ on this Cross' and continues:

> *Yet dare I almost be glad, I do not see*
> *That spectacle of too much weight for me.*
>
> . . . . .
>
> *Could I behold those hands which span the Poles,*
> *And turne all spheares at once, pierc'd with those holes?*
> *Could I behold . . .*
> *. . . that blood which is*
> *The seat of all our Soules, if not of his,*
> *Made durt of dust, or that flesh which was worne*
> *By God, for his apparell, rag'd, and torne?*
> *If on these things I durst not looke, durst I*
> *Upon his miserable mother cast mine eye,*
> *Who was God's partner here, and furnish'd thus*
> *Halfe of that Sacrifice, which ransom'd us?*[14]

Here with our Lord's Mother Crashaw takes his stand:

> *In shade of Death's sad tree*
> *Stood doleful she.*
>
> . . . . .
>
> *Before her eyes*
> *Hers and the whole World's Joy,*
> *Hanging all torn, she sees; and in His woes*
> *And pains, her pangs and throes:*
> *Each wound of His, from every part,*
> *All more at home in her one heart.*
>
> . . . . .
>
> *O teach these wounds to bleed*
> *In me; me, so to read*
> *This book of loves, thus writ*
> *In lines of death, my life may copy it*
> *With loyal cares.*
> *O let me, here, claim shares,*

> *Yield something in thy sad prerogative*
>   *(Great Queen of griefs!), and give*
> *Me too, my tears; who, though all stone,*
> *Think much that thou shouldst mourn alone.*
>
>   .   .   .   .   .
>
> *O teach mine (heart), too, the art*
> *To study Him so, till we mix*
> *Wounds, and become one crucifix.*[15]

Here are unquestioned sincerity, quiet intensity, restrained passion and many an exquisite line and graceful turn of fancy, but somehow we are not greatly moved. The emphasis is on externals such as we associate with a crucifix rather than with the Cross. We are called to sorrow as it might be before the bleeding corpse of Cæsar or the ashes of Joan of Arc. It needs mental effort and alert imagination to respond, and even then we fail, for all is so far away and so long ago. It is not easy to summon

> *tears of an antique bitterness.*[16]

We may even ask if the effort is worthwhile and what would be gained were we to achieve. It is in the providence of God that the physical sufferings of individuals, however profoundly they may have moved contemporaries, cannot long retain such power, or mankind would early have become de-humanized under an ever accumulating load of grief. The pristine horror of the thing cannot remain even with contemporaries.

> *Griefs, too, but brief while stay,*
>   *And sorrow, being o'er,*
> *Its salt tears shed away,*
>   *Woundeth the heart no more.*
> *Stealthily lave those waters*
>   *That solemn shore.*[17]

Think, for example, of De Stogumber, that burlesque

English chaplain of Mr. G. Bernard Shaw's *Saint Joan*, urging in his pseudo-patriotic, pseudo-religious fanaticism the burning of Joan, and, having witnessed the terrible scene, stumbling back agonized, half-demented, falling on his knees before Warwick and shrieking, 'O God, take away this sight from me! O Christ, deliver me from this fire that is consuming me! . . . I am in hell for evermore.'[18] But he was not. Probably Hell is never recognized as such in a man's early experience of it. Here was one who was not only a witness of the physical sufferings, but a prime instigator of them and a sharer in the guilt. Yet, years later, when we meet him in the Epilogue to the play, an old man and the beloved priest of an English country parish, he encounters the ghost of Joan—*and fails to recognize her*. He confesses, quite calmly, 'I did a very cruel thing once because I did not know what cruelty was like. . . . I have been a different man ever since, though a little astray in my wits sometimes.' There is no screaming agony as on the day of the execution. Indeed, he says, without emotion: 'She was burned to a cinder; dead and gone, dead and gone.' Just that! The tension of those first moments was too great to last. Human nature cannot bear it; but something is carried over and becomes a deposit in the personality and perhaps in the heritage of mankind for ever. What is it?

De Stogumber says, in the Epilogue, that because he had *seen* this cruel deed he was '*redeemed and saved*'. When Cauchon, a bishop of the Church who was at Joan's burning, makes the suggestion that the sufferings of Christ might have been enough to redeem and save him, De Stogumber rejects it vigorously: 'No. Oh, No: not at all. I had seen them in pictures and read of them in books, and been greatly moved by them, as I thought. But it was no use: *it was not our Lord that redeemed me, but a young woman whom I actually saw burned to death;* oh, most dreadful. *But it saved me.*'

One can well believe it, though such an effect is not necessarily universal. The simple, direct, emphatic sincerity of De Stogumber's words carries conviction. Joan's stake had, in that tremendous moment, blotted out for this professedly Christian man that Cross of Jesus before which he had so long prostrated himself in mechanical, uncomprehending, unavailing devotion. It had revealed to him a meaning which he had missed in that Cross: the horror of human wickedness and the tremendous power of suffering love and devotion to redeem. Apparently Joan's stake never lost its priority in this man's crucified mind, but that is of small account, since the inwardness of a greater Cross had thereby touched his heart and changed his life. God wrought salvation for him through that Cross at one remove.

Rarely in modern times, until Nazism and Fascism laid bloody hands on large sections of humankind, have people had to witness physical martyrdom deliberately inflicted. This being so it is more easily possible to stand before the Cross of Christ and see it, as De Stogumber did, as merely a crucifix; a reminder bodying forth in realistic and often crude art, 'old, unhappy, far-off things'. It is only when men come to see that Cross as, in his life thereafter, De Stogumber saw Joan's stake, that it ceases to be a crucifix and effects the miracle of redemption. 'It was dreadful . . . *but it saved me.*' Men have to pass through and beyond the mere physical 'dreadfulness' before they discover that saving power and grace.

That Crashaw is only or even mainly concerned with the physical sufferings of Jesus and the mental sufferings of the watchers by the Cross is inconceivable, prominently as these figure in his verse. He had himself undoubtedly passed

beyond the pain, beyond the broken clay,[19]

and assumes that his readers have done the same. He does not explain or help them to understand, but calls upon them to join him in general praise of his Lord.

Inevitably his poetry of the Passion directs us to one who was in certain respects his lyrical and spiritual descendant and with whom he repeatedly challenges comparison, Charles Wesley. Wesley, too, stands before the Cross and brings us there to note the wounds and physical sufferings of our Lord, but his references and descriptive touches are almost wholly incidental and are never far away from that interpretation of them which is the core of the Christian Faith. On one occasion, at least, he shares in thought with our Lord's mother the vigil at the Cross, expressing, as Crashaw does, the desire to be a partner in her sorrow. It is to *her* that Crashaw addresses his prayer:

> *Yea, let my life and me*
> *Fix here with three,*
> *And at the humble foot*
> *Of this fair tree* [*The Cross*], *take our eternal root.*
> *That so we may*
> *At least be in Love's way;*
> *And in these chaste wars, while the wing'd wounds flee*
> *So fast 'twixt Him and Thee,*
> *My breast may catch the kiss of some kind dart,*
> *Though as at second hand, from either heart.*[20]

In the corresponding passage, Charles Wesley also prays, but to *his* Lord:

> *Place us near the accursed wood*
> *Where Thou didst Thy life resign,*
> *Near as once Thy mother stood;*
> *Partners of the pangs divine,*
> *Bid us feel her sacred smart,*
> *Feel the sword that pierc'd her heart.*[21]

This mood is rare with Wesley. Not the physical sufferings of Jesus, long since over, inspire his mightiest Passion lines, but the eternal significance of them for sinful, suffering men. Rarely does he leave us gazing at a Crucifix. With Crashaw it is otherwise. Between us and the occasional glimpses he affords us of the meaning of our Lord's Passion there always hangs a diaphanous tapestry woven of blood and tears.

Thus, he gives a rendering of the hymn of St. Thomas Aquinas—*Ecce panis Angelorum: Adoro Te.*—so free that it virtually becomes his own:

> *O soft, self-wounding Pelican,*
> *Whose breast weeps balm for wounded man:*
> *Ah, this way bend Thy benign flood*
> *To a bleeding heart that gasps for blood.*
> *That blood, whose least drops sovereign be*
> *To wash my worlds of sins from me.*[22]

The introduction of the Pelican of fable, feeding its young with its own blood, jars upon us today, but it was for long a common emblem of Christ. For example, on meeting the spirit of St. John in Paradise, Beatrice says to Dante,

> *this is he who lay*
> *Upon the bosom of our Pelican.*[23]

Thus to symbolize the higher (and, in the case of Jesus, how much the higher!), by the lower, can hardly fail to be not only grotesque but irreverent to modern ears. In the verse just quoted, typical of others, there looms dim in the background little more than a shadow of the Divine purpose:

> *To wash my worlds of sins from me,*

whilst obtrusively in the foreground hangs the veil, heavily soaked in blood and tears. We are conscious of no sympathetically emotional response and having read we pass on to the sequel.

In such a hymn as Wesley's

> *For ever here my rest shall be*
> *Close to Thy bleeding side,*

there is the same symbolism of the shed blood which the writer combines with that of the feet washing—he has no manner of use for pelicans—and then breaks through and beyond it all, taking us with him and putting strong prayer not on our lips alone but in our hearts, for the hymn continues:

> *Sprinkle me ever with Thy blood,*
> *And cleanse, and keep me clean.*
>
> *Wash me, and make me thus Thine own,*
> *Wash me, and mine Thou art,*
> *Wash me, but not my feet alone,*
> *My hands, my head, my heart.*[24]

Wesley, however, can rise to greater heights than this and create more profound emotional effects, where the earthly symbols are utterly spiritualized in a purer and more exhilarating air. In that audacious hymn, 'With glorious clouds encompassed round', it is before no crucifix, no pelican, that he bids us stand and sing,

> *In manifested love* explain
>   *Thy wonderful design;*
> What meant *the suffering Son of Man,*
>   *The streaming blood divine?*
>
> . . . . .
>
> *Come then, and to my soul* reveal
>   *The heights and depths of grace,*
> *The wounds which all my sorrows heal,*
>   *That dear disfigured face.*[25]

The physical is but lightly touched upon; it is its meaning that matters and the stress lies on the moving petitions, 'Explain!', 'What meant?', 'Reveal!'. Even after such complete physical realism as

> *Five bleeding wounds He bears,*
>   *Received on Calvary,*

comes their significance in the purposes of God:

> *They pour effectual prayers,*
> *They strongly speak for me.*[26]

In lines that are more than usually reminiscent of Crashaw's realistic yearnings—

> *O let me kiss Thy bleeding feet,*
> *And bathe and wash them with my tears,—*

Wesley does not linger over the scene which he has so tenderly sketched, but goes straight to the universal message of the Cross:

> *The story of Thy love repeat*
> *In every drooping sinner's ears,*
> *That all may hear the quickening sound,*
> *Since I, even I, have mercy found.*[27]

There are occasions when the difference between the two writers in respect of this realism is emotional and more felt than capable of expression, as, for example, in Wesley's

> *Ah! show me that happiest place,*
> *The place of Thy people's abode,*
> *Where saints in an ecstasy gaze,*
> *And hang on a crucified God;...*
>
> *'Tis there I would always abide,*
> *And never a moment depart,*
> *Concealed in the cleft of Thy side,*
> *Eternally held in Thy heart.*[28]

There is a lightness, a delicacy of touch in this symbolism. It does not intrude and we feel the beating of a yearning heart beneath.

Hear him, too, in those cataclysmic Advent verses which found no place in the 1779 collection of hymns but appeared as No. 66 in its successor:

> *The dear tokens of His passion*
>   *Still His dazzling body bears;*
> *Cause of endless exultation*
>   *To His ransomed worshippers:*
> *With what rapture*
>   *Gaze we on those glorious scars!*[29]

Could anyone other than Charles Wesley have written that? 'His dazzling body!'—'Those glorious scars!' Only a supreme master of spiritual song could daringly and successfully fling out such phrases; the tyro would fail to the point of impiety. 'Those glorious *scars*!' One rejoices in the felicity and inevitability of the word. The 'bleeding wounds' are of the long ago, themselves the very *rationale* of the *Crucifix*; the 'scars' are the tokens, world without end, of the spiritual victory of the *Cross*, of Him who opened to mankind the gate of Eternal Life; the Lamb of God slain from the foundation of the world; an act less of Time than of Eternity.

Charles Wesley takes us into the arcana of the Christian Faith and bids us rejoice with him: 'Rejoice; again I say, Rejoice.' Crashaw leads us but to their threshold. Nevertheless, as we have noted, he himself had crossed that threshold, for his verse breathes throughout 'the peace and joy or faith'. Without doubt he meant almost all that Charles Wesley meant, but he lacked the latter's brilliant and moving power of expression. He gives the impression of a soul that has accepted simply and without reservation St. Paul's teaching that Christ has 'blotted out the bond that was against us by its ordinances, and hath taken it out of the way, nailing it to the cross'. '*Taken it out of the way,*' or, as Lightfoot suggests, 'put it out of sight'!—καὶ αὐτὸ ἦρκεν ἐκ τοῦ μέσου.[30] Thereafter sin has ceased to trouble him; even its ghost is for ever laid, if his poetry be a true witness. What few references there are to personal sin and guilt are elusive and seem to fade out into the thought of the general sinfulness of mankind. He addresses the Mother of our Lord thus:

> *Rich queen, lend some relief;*
> *At least an alms of grief,*
> To a heart who by sad right of sin
> Could prove the whole sum (too sure) due to him.[31]

In his fine *Hymn to the Name of Jesus* he includes himself with mankind:

> *we, dark sons of dust and sorrow,*

and

> *we, low worms,*

whilst in *Charitas Nimia* he asks:

> *Lord, what is man? why should he cost Thee*
> *So dear? What had his ruin lost Thee?*
> *Lord, what is man, that Thou hast over-bought*
> *So much a thing of nought?,*

and presently describes him as 'a piece of peevish clay'.

Such passages as these would scarcely merit quotation in the case of any other writer, but they are amongst the few and the strongest on this subject that Crashaw's verse affords. He is not directly concerned with sin: not even with the memory of it. Why, indeed, should he be? Some have felt this to be a defect. Sir Arthur Quiller-Couch suggests that 'Crashaw is often terribly at his ease in Zion'.[32] 'At ease,' yes! but why 'terribly'? It is an ease which St. Paul calls 'freedom', the freedom wherewith Christ makes men free: the freedom of a man who is no longer under *law*, but under *grace*. By what right or reason should we expect sin and sin's dis-ease to figure in the repertoire of every singer of spiritual things? Is it not, for the Christian, ἐκ τοῦ μέσου? This is not to suggest that Crashaw held his life to be one of sinless perfection; far from it. Rather it was a life in which sin was for ever being forgiven, through an ever-exercised faith in the Divine Life for ever being poured out before God. To this man Religion was Life and Freedom and his faith natural and instinctive; something beyond the dreary abstractions of debate. His soul was at one with Milton's angels:

> *O unexampled love,*
> *Love nowhere to be found less than Divine!*
> *Hail, Son of God, Saviour of men,* thy name
> Shall be the copious matter of my song
> Henceforth, *and never shall my harp thy praise*
> *Forget, nor from thy Father's praise disjoin.*[33]

Therefore his best verses sing and soar, carrying us with them, and they have that spontaneity which certainty and gladness alone can give, as they ring out repeatedly in praise of 'Jesus, the Name above every Name'.

> *I sing the Name which none can say*
> *But touch'd with an interior ray:*[34]

and in the very spirit of Watts's

> *Angels, assist our mighty joys,*
> *Strike all your harps of gold,*[35]

he summons Nature, Art, Music, to his aid: all

> *whose names belong*
> *Unto the everlasting life of song;*
>
> *Wake, lute and harp, and every sweet-lipped thing*
> *That talks with tuneful string:*
> *Start into life, and leap with me*
> *Into a hasty, fit-tuned harmony.*
>
> *Come, ye soft ministers of sweet sad mirth,*
> *Bring all your household-stuff of Heaven on earth;*
>
> *Cheer thee my heart!*
> *For thou too hast thy part*
> *And place in the great throng*
> *Of this unbounded all-embracing song.*

From this poem, *To the Name above every Name*, the Name

of Jesus, quotation is not easy. It stands among Crashaw's supreme achievements: a rushing, breathless exuberance of sheer, infectious music: a very cataract of praise; a Niagara of jubilation, that, when the surge and cadence of it are over, leaves the dazed, enchanted reader buoyant upon waves that dance and rock and sparkle, memories and motions of the impetuous flood that has borne him in its strong, exhilarating flow. When Crashaw says, 'Sing! Praise!', he who has music in his soul must perforce obey. So he sings and sings again the praise of Him Who

> *left His Father's Court, and came*
> *Lightly as a lambent flame,*
> *Leaping upon the hills, to be*
> *The humble King of you and me.*[36]

To no poem will the reader return with greater pleasure than to the one entitled *In the Holy Nativity of our Lord God. A Hymn Sung as by the Shepherds,* and written in the form of an Eclogue of Virgil. Two of St. Luke's shepherds contend in praise of the Infant Jesus and there is a directing Chorus. It is of interest to observe that Virgil's and Crashaw's shepherds are almost contemporaries. Virgil died in 19 B.C., before the Advent of the Child of Bethlehem, of whom his Fourth Eclogue is so curiously suggestive that it was at one time regarded as 'Messianic' and still is occasionally so described. Both groups of shepherds stand out against the one historical background of the Augustan Age. Crashaw even selects Virgilian names for St. Luke's shepherds: *Tityrus* from the First Eclogue and *Thyrsis* from the Seventh. There appears to be a slight measure of fitness in the choice, particularly in the case of Tityrus, who, as every reader of the Eclogues knows, is Virgil himself. Augustus, or Octavian as he then was, had promised land to the veterans of the Roman Army who had completed their term of service and he confiscated for that purpose estates already held by others. Virgil was amongst the unfortunates thus dispossessed, but at the instance of friends he obtained an audience of Octavian, who not only restored his land, but thereafter gave him his personal friendship. The songs of Tityrus in the eclogue are in praise of Octavian for his bounty and also descriptive of the visit to Rome. He puts Octavian (Augustus) on a level with the gods: 'for always shall he be a god to me'—*namque erit ille mihi semper deus.*[37]

It is of a far greater than Virgil's *deus* that Crashaw's Tityrus sings: one who is God Incarnate. Is there a reminiscence here of the *Divus Augustus*, the Emperor invested with divinity, but too late for Virgil's song? As we read we cannot fail to draw the contrast between the Ruler of the Roman world and Jesus born in a stable. That seems to be what Crashaw intended, for he himself hints at it when the chorus declares that in all the love and tenderness of His Mother, Jesus had 'more than Cæsar's birthright is'. Tityrus and Thyrsis are summoned to tell the sun that

> *he rises now, too late*
> *To show us aught worth looking at,*

for whilst he (the sun) slept, these men had

> *found out Heaven's fairer eye,*
> *And kissed the cradle of our King.*

The shepherds see the Infant Jesus as the Light of the World, eclipsing the brightness of the sun, and round that conception the poet lets his delicate, coruscating fancy play, in words whose sweet and artless beauty is perhaps unsurpassed by any who have made St. Luke's Incarnation story the theme of their song.

Hear, then, Tityrus!

> *Gloomy night embraced the place*
> *Where the noble Infant lay.*
> *The Babe looked up and showed His face;*
> *In spite of darkness, it was day.*
> *It was Thy day, Sweet, and did rise,*
> *Not from the East, but from Thine eyes.*

> *Poor world (said I), what wilt thou do*
> *To entertain this starry Stranger?*
>   *Is this the best thou canst bestow,*
> *A cold, and not too cleanly, manger?*
>   *Contend, the powers of Heaven and Earth,*
> *To fit a bed for this huge birth?*
>
>   *I saw the curled drops, soft and slow,*
> *Come hovering o'er the place's head;*
>   *Offering their whitest sheets of snow*
> *To furnish the fair Infant's bed;*
>   *Forbear, said I; be not too bold,*
> *Your fleece is white, but 'tis too cold.*

In unison both shepherds sing:

>   *We saw Thee in Thy balmy nest,*
> *Bright dawn of our eternal Day!*
>   *We saw Thine eyes break from their East,*
> *And chase the trembling shades away.*
>   *We saw Thee, and we blest the sight,*
> *We saw Thee by Thine Own sweet light.*

No reader of Crashaw can fail to be aware of Santa Teresa, and without reference to her no sketch of the poet would be either adequate or just. When he left England for the south of Europe, the Romance languages had long held for him the poetry of the world and his was the longing of Keats:

> *O for a beaker full of the warm south!*[38]

To France and Italy he went, but the joy of his desiring was Spain, and had it not been for

>   *fell death's untimely frost,*
> *That nipt my flower sae early,*[39]

thither he must have come at last. More, probably, than aught else, Spain meant for him Santa Teresa, that sane,

[53]

devout, cultured and austere mystic of the sixteenth century who still holds authority over those who come under her spell. The testimony of so devout and vigorous a mind as that of Dr. Alexander Whyte needs no other confirmation, though much might be given. 'Teresa's intellect', he writes, 'her sheer power of mind, is enough of itself to make her an intensely interesting study to all thinking men'; and he goes on to quote Bishop Palafox:

What I admire in her is the peace, the sweetness, and the consolation with which in her writings she draws us toward the best, so that we find ourselves captured rather than conquered, imprisoned rather than prisoners. No one reads the Saint's writings who does not presently seek God, and no one through her writings seeks God who does not remain in love with the Saint.[40]

These are impressive words, strong to send the reader to Teresa herself. Crashaw was 'in love with the Saint' and lived in this enchantment, three of his poems being the creation of its witchery. The first of them, *A Hymn, to the Name and Honour of the Admirable Saint Teresa*, he prefaces by a brief personal tribute: 'a woman for angelical height of speculation, for masculine courage and performance more than a woman.' When a child of six, Teresa had fervently desired martyrdom, thus the sooner to enter into her Saviour's presence, and to that end had attempted an escape from home in search of the land of the Moors, hopeful that these enemies of Christianity would oblige her and thus ensure for her the martyr's crown. This incident made an impression upon Crashaw such as would evoke the contemptuous pity of almost any amateur psychologist today, but that need not detract from our pleasure in the poem. The poet himself, we remember, had been moved by a kindred emotion in his contemplation of the Cross. He sees this, her desire, not as a mental obliquity due to irrational upbringing, but as a sign of a preternatural sanctity. Like Abraham's willingness to sacrifice Isaac, it is counted to her for righteousness, but the act itself is averted by the power of God.

> *She'll to the Moors; and trade with them*
> *For this unvalued diadem* [her life]:
> *She'll offer them her dearest breath,*
> *With Christ's name in't, in change for death:*
> *She'll bargain with them, and will give*
> *Them God, teach them how to live*
> *In Him; or, if they this deny,*
> *For Him she'll teach them how to die.*
> *So shall she leave amongst them sown*
> *Her Lord's blood, or at least her own.*
>
> . . . . .
>
> *Farewell house, and farewell home!*
> *She's for the Moors, and martyrdom.*

Coleridge regarded Crashaw's lines to St. Teresa as his finest work and wrote of the passage just quoted:

> These verses were ever present to my mind whilst writing the second part of *Christabel*; if, indeed, by some subtle process of the mind they did not suggest the first thought of the whole poem.[41]

But the martyr's crown is not for her;

> *wise Heaven will never have it so,*

and she has to return

> *t' embrace a milder martyrdom.*

Before her lies a life of strenuous earthly toil and many are the deaths she must die, but there shall be easeful triumph at the last, as

> *Heav'n opens wide*
> *Her ever-during gates, harmonious sound*
> *On golden hinges moving.*[42]

> *Angels, thy old friends, there shall greet thee,*
> *Glad at their own home now to meet thee.*
>   *All thy good works which went before*
> *And waited for thee, at the door,*
> *Shall own thee there; and all in one*
> *Weave a constellation*
> *Of crowns, with which the King thy Spouse*
> *Shall build up thy triumphant brows.*
>   *All thy old woes shall now smile on thee,*
> *And thy pains sit bright upon thee,*
> *All thy sorrows here shall shine,*
> *All thy sufferings be divine:*
> *Tears shall take comfort, and turn gems,*
> *And wrongs repent to diadems.*

Finally, he sees her attended in Heaven by the souls spiritually begotten of her on earth. She and they approach the Ultimate Divine Presence and Crashaw urges her forward in words of simple and fervent beauty:

>   *Go now*
> *And with them all about thee, bow*
> *To Him; put on (He'll say), put on*
> *(My rosy love) that thy rich zone*
> *Sparkling with the sacred flames*
> *Of thousand souls, whose happy names*
> *Heaven keeps upon thy score: (Thy bright*
> *Life brought them first to kiss the light,*
> *That kindled them to stars,) and so*
> *Thou with the Lamb, thy Lord, shalt go,*
> *And wheresoe'er He sets His white*
> *Steps, walk with Him those ways of light,*
> *Which who in death would live to see,*
> *Must learn in life to die like thee.*

Crashaw calls his second *Teresa* poem an Apology for the first. The enmity that then existed between Spain and an England that still remembered the Great Armada and events that led to its sailing had no power to lessen his admiration of the Saint, for

> *Souls are not Spaniards too: one friendly flood*
> *Of Baptism blends them all into a blood.*
> *Christ's Faith makes but one body of all souls,*
> *And Love's that body's soul; no law controls*
> *Our free traffic for Heaven;* we may maintain
> Peace, sure, with piety, though it come from Spain.
> *What soul soe'er in any language, can*
> *Speak Heav'n like hers, is my soul's countryman.*
> *O 't is not Spanish, but 't is Heav'n she speaks.*

The third of these poems, entitled *The Flaming Heart: upon the Book and Picture of the Seraphical Saint Teresa as she is usually expressed with a seraphim beside her*, has the distinction of containing some of Crashaw's most irritating lines and bizarre fancies and also what is generally regarded as his most magnificent flight of unfettered eloquence. A Seraph is the recognized emblem of Teresa, and the poet takes to task a painter who has depicted one in her company. 'You must', he adjures the reader,

> *transpose the picture quite,*
> *And spell it wrong to read it right;*
> *Read him for her and her for him,*
> *And call the saint the seraphim.*

The road by which he then leads us in trying to effect this transformation is tortuous, bewildering, and rather boring. Suddenly there is a startling change, as though he had, in a moment's gift of almost miraculous strength, flung off all restraint, to riot superbly in a new-found freedom. Gone all striving for effects that wilt even in the moment of their unfolding; gone all verbiage, all false sentiment, and as though she had power in Heaven to prevail with God on his behalf, he cries to this woman, who has possessed his spirit with her own:

> *O thou undaunted daughter of desires!*
> *By all thy dower of lights and fires;*
> *By all the eagle in thee, all the dove;*
> *By all thy lives and deaths of love;*
> *By thy large draughts of intellectual day,*
> *And by thy thirsts of love more large than they;*
> *By all thy brim-fill'd bowls of fierce desire,*
> *By thy last morning's draught of liquid fire;*
> *By the full kingdom of that final kiss*
> *That seized thy parting soul, and seal'd thee His;*
> *By all the Heaven thou hast in Him*
> *(Fair sister of the seraphim!)*
> *By all of Him we have in thee;*
> *Leave nothing of myself in me.*
> *Let me so read thy life, that I*
> *Unto all life of mine may die.*

Wordsworth's salutation to Milton,

> *Thy soul was like a star and dwelt apart,*[43]

might, with equal truth though various meaning, have been addressed to Crashaw. His was the sequestered spirit that shuns life's hurly-burly; the cloistered soul that finds its strength and joy within. Christ is there: that real Church which is the Kingdom of God is there; and thankfully he accepts what they offer—*and enjoys it*. Herein is life. Religion is his world and its ambrosia suffices him. In lines addressed to a girl to whom he had given a prayer-book he describes in a few words the society of his day as it appeared to him.

> *Say, gentle soul, what can you find*
> *But painted shapes,*
> *Peacocks and apes,*
> *Illustrious flies,*
> *Gilded dunghills, glorious lies;*
> *Goodly surmises*
> *And deep disguises,*
> *Oaths of water, words of wind?*

> *Truth bids me say 'tis time you cease to trust*
> *Your soul to any son of dust.*[44]

He sees the world as Francis Quarles saw it and finds there nothing to tempt him, so he shuts his door upon it all and keeps inviolate the sanctuary of his soul, with the incomparable treasures therein.

Unheroic? perhaps!—and perhaps not! Remember! He had been bruised and battered by circumstances not of his making; a perverse world had blighted his hopes, cheated him of his dues, and hounded him from his academic cloister, haunt of a perhaps too self-centred peace. He had contemptuously acquiesced and—he died at thirty-six. It is unkind and unwise to pass severe judgement upon a life only half complete. His loyalties led him along chequered ways of earthly poverty, discomfort and apparent futility. By human standards his life petered out in failure, yet, in the winter of his adversity when no bird note pierced the frost-bound air, he maintained that immaculacy of the spirit which is more than a counterpoise to life's ills. To the untimely end he remained the 'self-remembering soul' of his own verse, that

> *sweetly recovers*
> *Her kindred with the stars; not basely hovers*
> *Below; but meditates her immortal way*
> *Home to the original source of Light and intellectual day.*[45]

IV

The Scrutiny of the Soul

Sir John Davies—1569-1626

ONE EVENING toward the end of the year 1597 or in the beginning of 1598, as dinner was proceeding in the Hall of the Middle Temple, the door was flung open and a young man marched in, armed with a dagger, defying convention by wearing a hat, and accompanied by two persons carrying swords. Proceeding to the barristers' table, the intruder drew a cudgel from beneath his gown and broke it over the head of Richard Martin, one of the diners. Then, facing his victim and flourishing a sword above his head, he executed a kind of war-dance at the bottom of the room and hastily withdrew from before the astonished and bewildered assembly, to escape by boat.

To this so unpromising incident we owe one of the outstanding didactic poems of our literature, *Nosce Teipsum*. Its author was John Davies, the youthful aggressor of the Middle Temple, destined later to move in the broad spaces of public life and to enjoy the favour of Court and State. He was born at Tisbury, in Wiltshire, in 1569. His father died in 1580 and his mother, left in sole charge of him and his two brothers, 'brought them upp all to learning'. John went to Winchester School and New College, Oxford, and became a commoner of Queen's College in 1585. In 1587 he was admitted to the Middle Temple. The death of his mother seems to have inaugurated a period of youthful dissipation, but his studies did not share the neglect that overtook his morals. A friendship developed between him and the aforesaid Richard Martin, who was later to become the Recorder of the City of London. The chastisement scene was probably the sequel to sarcasms directed by Martin, when in a state of intoxication, against his friend Davies.

By the unanimous sentence of his judges, John Davies was 'disbarred' for his offence. He had been called to the Bar three years previously. The sentence meant the withdrawal of all his rights and privileges, thus depriving him of his means of livelihood. For a man of twenty-nine, fully qualified after long and costly training, this was a highly serious and sobering situation, and to take stock of it in all its bearings he withdrew to the seclusion of Oxford. So sincere was his subsequent repentance and so genuine his pledge of future good conduct that in 1601 he was permitted to make his apologies to those whom he had offended, was reinstated and allowed to retain his seniority.

There ensued a life of exacting and devoted service. When, on the death of Queen Elizabeth, James Stuart proceeded in state from Scotland to assume the crown of England, John Davies was in his escort. The new king appointed him Solicitor-General for Ireland, and on his arrival in that country in 1603 he was knighted. Ireland was then, as ever, the Cassandra of British statesmen, her 'ancestral voices prophesying war'[1] as vigorously and uncompromisingly as in the past, and Davies gave himself without reserve to study the complex situation and to devise ameliorative treatment. It is upon his work in Ireland that his political reputation chiefly rests, and his reports on Irish affairs were long valued for their outstanding merit.

In 1619 he returned to England and sat in the House of Commons as member for Newcastle-under-Lyme. In 1626 he was suddenly struck down by apoplexy and passed away before he could assume the office of Chief Justice to which he had been appointed.

Sir John Davies married Lady Eleanor, a daughter of the Earl of Castlehaven. Their daughter, Lucy, married

Ferdinando, the Sixth Earl of Huntingdon. Through that marriage Davies become a great-grandfather of Theophilus, the Ninth Earl, who married Selina, second daughter of Earl Ferrers: that Countess of Huntingdon so famous in the Methodist Revival and the Calvinistic controversies of the eighteenth century. Lady Margaret Hastings, a sister of the Ninth Earl, and therefore a great-granddaughter of John Davies, married Benjamin Ingham, in his youth an 'Oxford Methodist', who later left both Methodism and the Established Church, of which he was an ordained minister, to found an 'Inghamite Connexion' in the North of England.

Was John Wesley aware of these connecting links between Sir John Davies and Methodism? Probably not; but they would have been of undoubted interest to him, for he held Sir John's work in very high regard.

We are not here concerned with the public life of John Davies, but with that period of exile in Oxford, lasting almost four years, that ensued upon his loss of the privileges and fellowship of the Temple. According to Xenophon, the more his hero, Cyrus, pondered a certain situation, 'the more he felt *the need of leisure*, if he were to deal worthily with the highest matters'.[2] It is a need more often recognized than met, and, lo! by the unlikely road of egregious folly, leisure had come to Davies, and that of a quality and duration such as he would neither have expected nor freely sought, and he used it 'to deal worthily with the highest matters'. He was a lawyer and looked at life with the clarity of Edmund in *King Lear*:

This is the excellent foppery of the world, that, when we are sick in fortune—often the surfeit of our own behaviour—we make guilty of our disasters the sun, the moon, and the stars: as if we were villains by necessity: fools by heavenly compulsion.[3]

For Davies there was to be no such 'excellent foppery'. He saw the folly of his ways and sought neither planetary nor other scapegoat. In his writing he stands up to his punishment without resentment or sense of injury, nor ever urges the familiar petition: 'Turn from us all those evils that we most righteously have deserved.'[4] Having reviewed the course of his life, he emerges a man acquiescent in the justice of his own condemnation, and in a newly acquired possession of his own soul, resolved now to

> *teach high thought, and amiable words,*
> *And courtliness . . .*
> *And love of truth, and all that makes a man.*[5]

He had undergone a kind of spiritual conversion, in which the mind played a greater part than the emotions, and that at least makes for stability. Out of his contrition and new self-possession sprang *Nosce Teipsum*, witnessing how, on occasion, 'sweet are the uses of adversity'.

In the thirty-eighth and following stanzas the poem is definitely linked to the writer's recent experiences. Having discovered some of the values latent in affliction, he writes:[6]

> *If ought can teach us ought, Afflictions lookes,*
> *(Making us looke into our selves so neere,)*
> *Teach us to know our selves beyond all bookes,*
> *Or all the learned Schooles that ever were.*
>
> *This mistresse lately pluckt me by the eare,*
> *And many a golden lesson hath me taught;*
> *Hath made my senses quicke, and Reason cleare,*
> *Reformed my Will and rectifide my thought.*

In consequence he had been moved honestly to face the fact of his own being and to search out its implications.

> *My selfe am center of my circling thought,*
> *Onely my selfe I studie, learne, and know.*

One of his discoveries is that the spirit of the natural man is fashioned for a freedom that it does not enjoy; fettered in an environment less spacious than its powers demand.

> *I know my* Soule *hath power to know all things,*
> *Yet is she blinde and ignorant in all;*
> *I know I am one of Nature's little kings,*
> *Yet to the least and vilest things am thrall;*

—a stanza, incidentally, which John Wesley quotes with slight inaccuracy in his sermon on 'The Deceitfulness of the Human Heart'[7]—

> *I know my life's a paine and but a span,*
> *I know my* Sense *is mockt with every thing:*
> *And to conclude, I know my selfe a* man,
> *Which is a* proud, *and yet a* wretched *thing.*

This legacy of knowledge from his earlier life was both self-revealing and disconcerting, but in his solitude he made the compensatory discovery of the kingliness inherent in his manhood; that Reason and Understanding which Marcus Aurelius held to be 'a fragment of God Himself'.

We are not surprised when John Davies reaches back through the centuries and boldly appropriates one of the profoundest sayings of the ancient world to serve as title for his poem. Written over the portico of the Temple of Delphi, in letters of gold, were words which some have professed to regard as the quintessence of human wisdom: γνῶθι σεαυτὸν: *Know thyself*: in its Latin form, *Nosce Teipsum*. They are more than a command; they are a revelation to man of his duty as an intelligent being. They have been ascribed to more than one outstanding individual of antiquity: amongst others to Pythagoras, to Thales, and, in particular, to Socrates, although the Platonic Socrates, in the *Protagoras*, tells how certain admirers of the Spartan scheme of education, 'having met together, consecrated the first-fruits of their wisdom to Apollo in the Temple of Delphi, inscribing those sentences which all men have in their mouths: γνῶθι σεαυτὸν and μηδὲν ἄγαν'.[8]*
Juvenal probably comes nearest to the truth in regarding

* Nothing in excess.

the injunction as a kind of 'word of the Lord' to mankind in general: *E coelo descendit* γνῶθι σεαυτόν.[9] The 'revelation' must surely have come independently and even simultaneously to many a thinking mind, but not all men become vocal when 'The Word' descends upon them, which may be one of the uncovenanted mercies of God.

If, however, the words have increased compelling power over us as we associate them with some outstanding name, let us be free to choose our own. Robert Bridges selected Socrates and one feels the entire fitness thereof; there is a glamour about the name that adds prestige to the ancient words. Clearly this association helped to inspire the thought of the poet, for in his *Testament of Beauty* Bridges hails Socrates as a pioneer of human progress, who cleared away much of the jungle growth that was impeding men in their advance to a knowledge of right personal relations and moral qualities, so that now

> *all enter free*
> *at the great clearing made by Socrates of yore,*
> *when he said,* Know thyself: *for true to his chief premiss*
> *that ignorance is the root of all men's folly, he taught*
> *to turn the lamp of Reason inwardly upon the mind.*
> *And truly with that keen* Γνῶθι σεαυτόν *of his*
> *was great felling of trees.*[10]

Felling of trees! A light- and health-giving activity! and among the trees that need to be felled, the jungle growths of the mind, is that of a spurious self-knowledge; such self-knowledge, for example, as expects to find satisfaction for real or fancied wrongs in breaking cudgels on the heads of offending people; or the spurious knowledge that takes pride in a self that is flattering to a certain type of human vanity, but is afraid to examine it too rigorously lest it melt 'into air, into thin air'. There is something of the charming Fanny Squeers in most of us, 'looking in her own little glass, where . . . she saw, not herself, but the reflection of some pleasant image in her own brain'.[11] It was *her own little glass,* you observe: clearly, a distorting mirror. A plain surface we can none of us obtain, nor, perhaps, could tolerate. There are, however, degrees of distortion and self-deception, and many reflections are of graver import than that which Fanny greeted with her 'nods, and becks, and wreathed smiles'. Walt Whitman looked in *his* mirror and saw . . . GOD! for most people, surely, a sufficiently staggering experience! He is noisily cheerful about it but sufficiently charitable to see God in other faces as well:

> *In the faces of men and women I see God,*
> *and in my own face in the glass:*[12]

which may be a dangerous delusion or just one extravagantly polished facet of ultimate truth. All depends upon Walt Whitman and what he meant. A man needs a select audience before which to scatter promiscuously such sweeping subtleties, and even then, if he is wise, he will both curb his generous instincts and be more explicit.

Nothing, not God, is greater to one than one's self,[13]

he continues: a remark which may be either flippant or profound. In so far as it expresses a final satisfaction of Walt Whitman with Walt Whitman, the 'self' thus seen is a reflection more fantastic than that of Fanny Squeers. In so far as it is an attempt to understand personality in God and in man; in so far as it is the expression of an honest, religiously disposed, and philosophical mind, seeking to see things, not as they are or appear to be, but as they might or should be, and thus discovering the almost infinite potentialities of the human spirit; and in so far as what he sees humbles him to the very dust, the words express in deliberately extravagant fashion a self-knowledge which may carry a man far along the road that leads to God. Long before he arrives, the old *modus loquendi*, with its bombastic flavouring, will have become distasteful to his newly developed sensibilities, and he will want to state the old 'shewings', as Julian of Norwich would have called them, in a new way; perhaps more after the manner of Sir Thomas Browne, in the chaste beauty of prose written two hundred years before the robustious lines of Whitman:

> *There is surely a piece of Divinity in us, something that was before the Elements, and owes no homage unto the sun.*[14]

That is better, and when we read his words in the light of the cosmic ideas that were then beginning to fade in the dawn of modern scientific knowledge, they appear greatly daring in their suggestion of something in man that has power to force a passage through the four elements: earth, water, air, and fire; to bypass the spheres and all angelic hierarchies:

> *O'er heaven's high towers to force resistless way,*[15]

and so stand at last before 'the Great Spirit of the Universe', to claim a measure of kinship with Him.

'We feel that we are greater than we know.'[16] Thus, with even more becoming modesty, Wordsworth speaks for every man who looks upon himself and thinks; and when such a man makes the words his own we may be sure that he is facing toward the high places of life and that his feet are on the road of great discovery. This is the point that John Davies was approaching when, at the dictate of circumstance, he sat down to seek knowledge of himself. He, too, looked at his soul, but he found the sight, at first, almost beyond enduring: that soul

> *which did God's image beare,*
> *And was at first faire, good, and spotlesse pure,*

but whose beauties had now become so 'blotted' with her 'sinnes', that at the very sight of her reflection

> *she retires, and shrinkes for shame and feare.*

It is a good low-level station from which to set out for Paradise.

There was, however, a difficulty which Davies faced straight away: How is this self-knowledge to be obtained? Such a question, in his day, almost inevitably led to the introduction of Adam and Eve, Adam being the ethical 'whipping boy' of the Elizabethans as he had been for Christendom in general throughout the Middle Ages. The poem opens with forty-five stanzas which illustrate the attitude of the age to the Biblical account of the Creation and the Fall of Man. Most, even educated, men were still in bondage to the letter nor as yet escaped fully into the freedom of the idea. It must be remembered that the age of Davies was poised between the medieval and the modern worlds; hardly yet had men's thoughts and sensibilities begun to disengage themselves from the Ptolemaic cosmology and to traffic with that which was being foreshadowed in the revolutionary simplifications of Copernicus. E. M. W. Tillyard points out that 'recent research has shown that the educated Elizabethan had plenty of text-books in the vernacular, instructing him in the Copernican astronomy, yet he was loth to upset the old order by applying his knowledge'.[17] So the old categories—Chaos and Cosmos, the 'Chain of Being', the Elements, the Spheres—were still tenacious in their grip on men's minds, and in the light of that fact the literature of the time must be read in order to be understood and appreciated. The mental climate was soon to change. When Milton put into the mouth of Raphael the questing, probing words,

> *what if the Sun*
> *Be centre to the world, and other stars,*
> *By his attractive virtue and their own*
> *Incited, dance about him various rounds?*,[18]

Ptolemy was becoming the shadow of a shade. John Davies, seventy years earlier, was certainly sensitive to the tremors that then threatened the once complacent integrity of the medieval cosmos, and expressed what one suspects to be resentment. In his earlier days he had written a poem, 'Orchestra', which is one of the most perfect expressions of the Elizabethan Age. Its subject matter is Dancing, and he treats it as one of the 'correspondencies' which the medieval mind loved to trace through all the planes of being. The Dances on the lower planes are resolved into the one, grand Dance of the Universe, moving to the 'cosmic harmony' or 'music of the spheres'. To the Elizabethan reader this would be commonplace. There were, however, certain sceptical individuals who refused to allow their minds to be lulled into inactivity by any such mythical harmonies, and to these Davies makes caustic allusion. One such, a far-away Pole named Nicolas Copernicus, had been dead fifty years, but his irreverent and disturbing theories had not died with him; they had spread and infected even Englishmen like William Gilbert, the royal physician, Francis Bacon, and many a lesser man endowed with the questing mind of an adventurous age. *A pox upon them all!* Davies seems to say: *Let the cosmic dance go on!*

> Onely the earth doth stand for ever still;
> Her rocks remove not nor her mountains melt;

But what will these godless, disturbing fellows, these intellectual busybodies, think of that? Dismiss them with a sneer!

> (Although some wits enricht with Learning's skill
>   Say heaven stands firme, and that the earth doth fleet,
>   And swiftly turneth underneath their feet)
> Yet though the earth is ever stedfast seen,
>   On her broad breast hath Dauncing ever beene.

A curious age, troubled by a vague sense of the impermanence of ancient customs and beliefs! A Prospero's Island from which a few discerning and courageous souls were escaping, some of them with the reluctance of Lot's wife; an Island whose misty enchantments were disappearing in the cold, clear dawn of a new intellectual day! In 1596, the year in which *Orchestra* was published, a delicate boy of eight years of age, the son of a bellicose parson, was living near Malmesbury in Wiltshire, bearing the commonplace name of *Thomas Hobbes*. In that same year a child was born near Poitiers in France, taking the name of *René Descartes*. The New Age was knocking at the door.

In his Elizabethan mansion, sturdy in his obstinacy, sits John Davies: not wholly deaf to the knocking, but determined to dwell as long as possible in the comfort of the medieval side of the door. There Adam and Eve are oracular for him, and in that far-away transaction in which they figured John Davies sees, of course, the origin of mankind's misery, which includes his own. In the instant of their creation and to the moment of their 'Fall' these two were the perfect expression of God's intentions towards men, for

> *God's hand had written in the hearts*
> *Of the first Parents, all the rules of good,*
> *So that their skill infusde did passe all arts*
> *That ever were, before, or since the Flood.*

John Earle, in his *Micro-cosmographie* (1628), illuminates the popular conception of Adam in his description of a child:

A child is a man in a small letter, yet the best copy of Adam before he tasted of Eve or the apple. . . . His soul is yet a white paper unscribbled with observations of the world, wherewith at length it becomes a blurred note-book. He is purely happy because he knows no evil, nor hath made means by sin to be acquainted with misery. He arrives not at the mischief of being wise, nor endures evils to come by foreseeing them.

Apparently it never occurred to Davies and the many who thought as he did that such a start for humanity may be a serious handicap, since it allows of no outlet to something better and precludes the very idea of progress. It can hardly be accounted a blessing when the conditions of life telescope the positive and superlative degrees of human excellence, squeezing out the comparative degree in the process, and so making impossible even the conception of a better and a best. Hardly can it be held a privilege that a man should start life at the very top of the tree, nurtured in some cosy, closely-woven nest, perched on

> *the topmost twig that looks up at the sky,*[19]

and without the power even to peep over its edge, to say nothing of leaving it; destined, therefore, apart from some cataclysmic happening, to remain for ever ignorant, not only that a tree upholds his nest of comfort, but that such things as trees and nests exist at all. To the normal onlooker there are only two alternatives to such a start: (1) to remain 'put', a difficult, if not impossible, accomplishment: continuing on a dead level of monotonous, unheroic goodness —the spurious righteousness of 'the topmost twig'—which must eventually act as an opiate to the soul; or (2) to change in the only direction left open, the downward one, and so to fall to levels on which men discover trees and a great many other things: all of them quite other than that perfect *best* with which they started, and where they may even arrive at a knowledge and experience of what is worst of all.

This 'perfection' in Adam and Eve was not, however, so complete as to render them immune to temptation from without. Nor was any Milton standing by, to croon soothingly above their nuptial couch,

> *sleep on,*
> *Blest pair, and O! yet happiest if ye seek*
> *No happier state, and know to know no more.*[20]

The mischief which was to reach cosmic dimensions began with a desire for knowledge, and now here is Davies himself, caught in the insidious toils of the same desire; the 'curse' is upon him; he wants *to know himself*, although he is quite clear in his own mind that

> desire to know *first made men fools,*
> *And did corrupt the root of all mankind.*

Had Matthew Prior been born a century earlier he would have had a timely word for John Davies:

> *Remember that the curs'd desire to know,*
> *Offspring of Adam, was thy source of woe.*
> *Why wilt thou then renew the vain pursuit,*
> *And rashly catch at the forbidden fruit?*
> *With empty labour and eluded strife*
> *Seeking by knowledge to attain to life;*
> *For ever from that fatal tree debarr'd,*
> *Which flaming swords and angry cherubs guard.*[21]

People who know only *Good* cannot know it *as good*, for knowledge of good *as such* implies knowledge of evil, which man's first parents had not got. In order, then, to effect the enlightenment of these primitive and 'perfect' people: in order that they might come to know *Good as Good*, there had to be a breaking in upon their goodness from without; they had to become aware of moral contrasts and contradictions. The attack begins:

> the Spirit of Lyes *suggests*
> *That they were blind, because they saw not ill;*

Ill! But what is this *ill* of which the enticing Spirit speaks? Here is a new word in the vocabulary of Paradise and there is nothing in their experience to which it corresponds. Assuredly there is something bewitching in the sound of it, like horns of some forbidden elfland 'faintly blowing'. Evil has begun its agelong enchantment of the spirit of man. They want to *know*.

Very ingeniously Davies depicts the Devil's difficulty. It was impossible for him to show them anything ill, evil, or even imperfect, so long as they and Creation with them remained 'unfallen'. Were not *all* God's works *good*? Again and again that judgement had gone forth as Creation had proceeded: 'God saw that it was good.' So

> *ill, being nought but a defect of good,*
> *In all God's works the Divell could not show*
> *While Man their lord in his perfection stood.*

Presently a possible solution of the problem shaped itself; these 'unfallen' lords of a perfect creation must *do* evil before they can *see* it; must themselves produce those contrasts that will open their eyes, making them 'as gods, knowing good and evil'. So, urged by 'the Spirit of Lyes',

> *themselves were first to doe the ill,*
> *Ere they thereof the knowledge could attaine;*
> *Like him that knew not poison's power to kill,*
> *Untill (by tasting it) himselfe was slaine.*

So they 'brought death into the world and all our woe'.

Nor did the majority of men question the literal historicity of it all for a moment. It was a transaction for which they found easy accommodation in what Professor J. Dover Wilson so delightfully calls 'the diminutive, compact, and tidy universe designed by Ptolemy fifteen hundred years before'.[22] Davies is not concerned, like Francis Quarles and John Milton, to linger over the forbidden fruit and 'the serpent, subtlest beast of all the field'. It is the consequence of all this, working itself out in the subsequent history of the race and in his personal history that interests him. All the outward as well as the inward world of those far-away people had become *different*; their 'knowledge of good bought dear by knowing ill'. It is that *different world*, still continued, into which St. Paul insisted that 'sin' had entered, that pulls Davies up in his rake's progress and compels him to ask: 'What is this all about? What sort of a creature am I? What *is* this *soul* which has inherited guilt, actually sinned and now suffers?'

Upon one element in this highly complex evil the mind of Davies fastens: ERROR.

> *Where they sought* knowledge *they did* error *find;*

and that is part of the 'Curse'. Further, they came to see

> *Those wretched shapes of* Miserie *and* Woe,
> *Of* Nakednesse, *of* Shame, *of* Povertie,
> *Which then their owne experience made them know,*

and a devastating bewilderment overtook them:

> *. . . then grew* Reason *darke, that* she *no more,*
> *Could the faire formes of* Good *and* Truth *discern;*
> Battes *they became, that* eagles *were before:*
> *And this they got by their* desire *to learne.*

The venture had miscarried and we, 'their wretched offspring', have inherited the same itch for knowledge and have to pay dearly for it, for

> Error *chokes the windowes of the minde,*

and 'Reason's Lamp' is now only a sparkle. We are far indeed from the initial, privileged position of our first parents:

> *How can we hope, that through the eye and eare,*
>   *This dying sparkle, in this cloudy place,*
>   *Can recollect these beames of knowledge cleere,*
>   *Which were infused in the first minds by grace?*

So Davies comes up against the ultimate barrier of unlimited ignorance which at one time or another has daunted and even depressed the most eager and inquiring minds. To that same barrier came Matthew Prior's *Solomon*, as he discovered

How narrow limits were to Wisdom given!
Earth she surveys; she thence would measure heaven:
Through mists obscure now wings her tedious way:
Now wanders, dazzl'd with too bright a day:
And, from the summit of a pathless coast,
Sees infinite, and in that sight is lost.[23]

Davies is haunted by the ghost of Socrates, the restless, pursy little man, who, having drunk his hemlock and arranged for the payment of his debts—a cock to Asclepius![24]—slipped the thread that bound him to Athens, to wander henceforward through all the ways of all the world, so long as the world shall endure, raising dead and dying *minds* to life. He is here in Elizabeth's England. His method is disconcerting but effective. Davies sees him as 'the wisest of all morall men', who said

He knew nought, but that he nought did know.

To that pause in his mental pilgrimage and to the realization that *omnia in mysterium exeunt* Davies appears to have come, as did many an Athenian of yore; like Euthydemus, for example, to whom Xenophon introduces us in the *Memorabilia*:[25] meeting Socrates on equal terms (usually a prelude to disaster!): settled in his opinions, but after his encounter with the philosopher constrained to admit: 'I am considering whether it would not be best for me to be silent, for I seem to know absolutely nothing'; and Xenophon quaintly adds: 'He went away, accordingly, in great dejection, holding himself in contempt, and thinking that he was in reality no better than a slave.' Well! It is excellent discipline for that kind of man. Earlier in their conversation Socrates had asked him if he had ever been to Delphi. 'Yes, *twice*,' was the reply. Euthydemus wished Socrates to know that he was no everyday sort of person: no conventional 'oncer' to Delphi. 'And did you observe', continued Socrates, 'what is written somewhere on the Temple wall, KNOW THYSELF?'

'I did,' replied Euthydemus. 'And did you take no thought of that inscription, or did you attend to it and try to examine yourself, to ascertain what sort of character you are?' Note his answer. 'I did not indeed try, for I thought that I knew very well already, since I could hardly know anything else if I did not know myself.' The arrogant fatuity of the man! Our fancy is tickled as we read again how 'he went away in great dejection . . . thinking that he was in reality no better than a slave'. He had at any rate discovered one truth about himself and had learned more in his encounter with Socrates than his two visits to Delphi had taught him.

Among the *logia* of Jesus discovered at Oxyrhynchus is one that is particularly illuminating. The text is very imperfect, but there is substantial agreement among those who have attempted restoration. M. R. James, in his *Apocryphal New Testament*, gives that of Lagrange:

Jesus saith . . . the kingdom of heaven is within you and whosoever knoweth God shall find it; for if ye know him ye shall know yourselves and shall know that ye are sons of the Father that is perfect: and likewise ye shall know yourselves to be citizens in heaven.[26]

If that is not exactly what Jesus said it might very well have been, so reminiscent is it of sayings of his recorded in the canonical Gospels. Here knowledge of God is the key to knowledge of self, but knowledge of that self in a new and liberating relationship. Truly to know God is to know His Kingdom, or Rule, within: to see the 'self' as a 'tabernacle' of God is to know oneself in a new way, as a self that belongs to God in the peculiarly intimate relation of 'indwelling'.

> *The outward God he findeth not*
> *Who finds not God within.*

It is this knowledge of himself that Davies is approaching. He is disturbed as he sees how men strive after knowledge of outward things and are content to remain ignorant of the

Self within and its relationship to God. In the region of Law, for example, where he himself was so much at home,

> *We interpret lawes, which other men have made,*
> *But reade not those which in our hearts are writ.*

For this ignorance Davies gives what is clearly for him a convincing reason:

> *. . . . she* [*the soul*] *is so corrupt, and so defac't,*
> *As her owne image doth her selfe affright.*
>
> Man's Soule *which did God's image beare,*
> *And was at first faire, good, and spotless pure;*
> *Since with her sinnes her beauties blotted were,*
> *Doth of all sights her owne sight least endure.*

We are far away from the complacency of a Walt Whitman here, a complacency without wings; for when a man looks at himself and can see only God, there is no empyrean for his conquering. On the contrary, the man whom Davies has in mind sinks into a limbo of self-forgetfulness and spiritual disintegration; his soul

> *Turnes from her selfe and in strange things delites.*

Here are the two extremes from which the wise man seeks to be delivered.

So Davies comes nearer to his main theme: *Of the Soule of Man and the Immortalitie thereof.*[27] The words 'self' and 'soul' are interchangeable as he uses them, which is clear from such a stanza as

> *That* Power *which gave me eyes the World to view,*
> *To see my selfe infused an inward light;*
> *Whereby my* Soule, *as by a mirror true,*
> *Of her owne forme may take a perfect sight.*

What is the *Soul* of whose immortality he seeks assurance? Briefly he reviews the speculations in which men have indulged from ancient to modern times, but to him it is folly and perversity to seek an answer that omits all reference to God, for

> Thou *which didst* Man's soule *of nothing make,*
> *And when to nothing it was fallen agen,*
> *To make it new, the forme of man didst take,*
> *And* God *with* God, *becam'st a* Man *with men:*

Thou, that has fashioned twice this Soule *of ours*
 So that she is by double title Thine;
 Thou onely knowest her nature and her powers,
 Her subtill forme Thou onely canst define.

So he dismisses the *a priori* philosophers. To know oneself is a task impossible apart from Divine enlightenment, and he boldly declares:

The soule a substance, *and a* spirit *is,*
 Which God *Himselfe doth in the body make;*
 Which makes the Man: *for every man from this,*
 The nature *of a* Man, *and* name *doth take.*

And though this spirit be to the body knit,
 As an apt meane her powers to exercise;
 Which are life, motion, sense, *and* will, *and* wit,
 Yet she survives, although the body dies.

With that final line the text which the poet seeks to expound and never forgets comes more clearly into view. He might fittingly have prefaced his poem with two lines from the epitaph of Abbot Alcuin, then eight centuries dead:

> *Quapropter potius animam curare memento,*
> *Quam carnem, quoniam haec manet, illa perit.*[28]

The two last quoted stanzas are a preliminary and far from comprehensive summary of what is to follow. Davies goes on to expound his thesis in a series of propositions expressed with Euclidean exactness and brevity:

> *That the Soule is a Thing subsisting by it Selfe without the Body.*
> *That the Soule is more than a Perfection or Reflection of the Sense.*
> *That the Soule is more than the Temperature of the Humors of the Body.*
> *That the Soule is a Spirit.*
> *That it cannot be a Body.*
> *That the Soule is created immediately by God.*

What earlier writers meant by the *Soul* need not concern us here, but what the Elizabethans meant is all-important. There were the 'humours', four liquids produced by the action of the liver upon food. It was held that when these existed in the right proportions the body was perfectly healthy. They were physiological rather than psychological, but they were believed to have psychological effects, and Davies 'proves' that the Soul is more than merely their temperature. It is sufficient for our purpose to note that inasmuch as the 'humours' have long been consigned to whatever place is appointed for the reception of the discarded hypotheses of science—which must be a roomy one—we need not concern ourselves with this part of the poem. We are, however, concerned with the Elizabethan view of man's higher faculties. These were regarded as seated in the brain and as existing in three orders. The highest of all was the Reason, which served both to distinguish man from the beasts and to unite him with God. This Reason was in two parts: (*a*) the Wit, or, as we should call it today, the Understanding, and (*b*) the Will. Reason *knows* or *understands* and then *wills* or *acts*; the Will is Reason's executive arm. The second order consisted of (*a*) Common Sense, (*b*) Fancy or Imagination, and (*c*) Memory. These were ministered to by the members of the third and lowest order, viz., the five senses, Sight, Hearing, Touch, Taste, and Smell, which stimulated Common Sense, Fancy, and Memory by providing material on which they could work. These last, in turn, served up the result to Reason, whose office it was to co-ordinate it and bring it into effective service. This is not technical psychology but merely a picturesque statement of the familiar processes of knowing, willing, and acting. It has the advantage of being unembarrassed by freshly-minted and hard visaged technical words. Like many much more sententious statements it *describes* but does not *explain*.

It is this unifying Reason, then, which distinguishes man from the brute creation and this is amply illustrated in the literature of the time, such as the speech of Arbaces to Althea, in the Beaumont and Fletcher play, *A King and No King*:

> *Know, I have lost,*
> *The only difference betwixt man and beast,*
> *My reason.*[29]

Divines like Jeremy Taylor stressed it in their sermons:

If we consider what the soul is in its own capacity to happinesse, we shall find it to be an excellency greater than the sun; of al angelicall substance, sister to a cherubin, and image of the divinity, and the great argument of that mercy whereby God did distinguish us from the lower form of beasts and trees and minerals,[30]

and in his famous *Aphorisms* Benjamin Whichcote notes that

There is nothing proper and *peculiar* to Man; but the Use of Reason and Exercise of Virtue.[31]

Socrates would probably have simplified this by remarking that the latter is a necessary consequence of the former.

John Davies insists on the separate existences of body and soul, a distinction which John Wesley uses in one of his letters to illustrate the nature of the Sacrament of Baptism: 'The outward sign is no more a part of the inward grace than the body is a part of the soul.'[32] The body is as the sacramental bread and wine to the soul; the outward and visible sign of the recondite, invisible reality, the Soul of Man. In true classical fashion Davies regards this Soul as feminine:

> She is a substance, *and a reall thing,*
> *Which hath it selfe an actuall working might;*
> *Which neither from the Senses' power doth spring,*
> *Nor from the bodie's humors, tempred right.*

So stands the soul of man in the Elizabethan scheme of psychology; independent for its existence both of the senses and 'humours' of the body. In all this John Davies keeps very near to Platonic doctrine. When the soul exercises choice, memory, foresight and imagination, and divines cause and effect,

> *These actions in her closet all alone,*
> *(Retired within her selfe) she doth fulfill;*
> *Use of her bodie's organs she hath none,*
> *When she doth use the powers of Wit and Will.*

Perhaps at this point the shade of Thomas Aquinas tapped him on the shoulder and whispered:

Don't forget, my little philosopher, that in our neatly ordered and orthodox Christendom Plato cannot have all things his own way. Don't forget how I have established that the soul is not complete in itself; that it is an integral part of that composite entity we call Man, and can only, at this stage of its existence, realize itself fully when in union with the matter of the body.

Davies has to admit this. The soul may, indeed, have an independent existence, but, in this sphere of being, that can count for little apart from the body and its sense organs. He seems to admit it grudgingly, like a true Platonist, regarding the body as the soul's prison. This august prisoner is cut off from the outer world and can only regard it through the windows of his cell, the sense organs of the body. Davies does not face the alternative: the prison walls broken down, viz., the body destroyed, and the soul thus left free to range through the outer world at will, gaining—by what means?—immediate instead of mediated knowledge.

> *Yet in the bodie's prison so she lies,*
> *As through the bodie's windowes she must looke,*
> *Her divers powers of sense to exercise,*
> *By gathering notes out of the World's great book.*
>
> *Nor can her selfe discourse or judge of ought,*
> *But what the Sense collects and home doth bring;*

(For that he deserves an approving smile from the *Angelical Doctor*.)

> *And yet the power of her discoursing thought,*
> *From these collections, is a divers thing.*

We must remember that Davies is concerned to establish the *Immortality* of the Soul, and therefore he has to guard against any theory of the soul's connexion with the body that would involve the dissolution of the former in that of the latter. The Orphic doctrine that the body is the tomb of the soul was probably too suggestive of extinction to attract him. The later Platonic 'prison-house' theory serves him better, as expressed, for example, in the *Phaedrus*, where Plato regards the 'self' as 'Imprisoned like an oyster in its shell'.[33] It was also a view favoured by the Stoics. 'O my soul, my soul!' wails Marcus Aurelius, 'wilt thou never attain to goodness and simplicity, oneness and nakedness, and shine through the bars of thy bodily prison?'[34] It was, indeed, with one modification or another, a popular view of the time and will probably long continue because of its undoubted usefulness. There was Edmund Waller, for example (1606–87), to whom the body was

> *The soul's dark cottage, battered and decayed;*[35]

for Time and the 'Weather' of life have dilapidating powers

and in that climax of their assaults which we call 'death' they effect the soul's release. Henry Vaughan's 'prison' (1622–95) was the chrysalis:

> *But when time's restless wave*
> *Their substance doth deprave,*
> *And the more noble Essence finds his house*
> *Sickly, and loose,*
> *He, ever young, doth wing*
> *Unto that spring,*
> *And source of spirits, where he takes his lot,*
> *Till time no more shall rot*
> *His passive Cottage.*[36]

Jeremy Taylor (1613–67) is crystal clear on the popular view:

WE know ... that the body is a prison and the soul is in fetters while we are alive; and that when the body dies the Soul springs and leaps from her Prison, and enters into the first liberty of the Sons of God.[37]

John Davies was dead when Jeremy Taylor wrote that, but it may well have been that his poem fortified the great preacher in his faith. In the thought of Davies the Soul is indeed a prisoner, but, we note, not one serving a judicial sentence; rather one that is its own master within the limits of its confinement, making its decisions and issuing its orders on the strength of the information conveyed through those sense organs which are its guardians and its couriers rather than its gaolers.

Davies sees evidence that the soul is distinct from the body in the independence of the former of Space and Time. Regarding Space, he cites the visual memory as 'proof' that the soul is bigger than the body:

> *what vast body must we make the* mind
> *Wherein are men, beasts, trees, towns, seas, and lands;*
> *And yet each thing a proper place doth find,*
> *And each thing in the true proportion stands?*

Davies does not pause to distinguish between location in memory or imagination and location in extended space, but inquires how this 'phenomenon' of the greater within the less may be accounted for. His answer has a modern ring: it is by *sublimation*. The soul

> *turnes*
> *Bodies to spirits, by* sublimation *strange.*
>
> *From their grosse* matter *she abstracts the* formes,
> *And drawes a kind of* quintessence *from things.*

In other words, as he presently explains, the soul

> *from things* particular,
> ... *doth abstract the* universall *kinds;*
> *Which bodilesse and immateriall are,*
> *And can be lodged but onely in our minds,*

and from 'divers accidents and acts' arrives at abstract ideas like 'Nature, Fortune, and the Vertues'. So we are back again with Plato, who, indeed, throughout the poem, is never far away. It is *Universals* to which memory and imagination give existence in the spirit realm of the soul or mind. That is true, and a non-Platonist or Nominalist would retort that they exist nowhere else and that their existence is non-spatial. Davies does not appear to have been at all disconcerted by the fact that *Particulars* also exist in memory; that, indeed, it is out of those particulars that the universal or general notion is built up, as Socrates and Aristotle, but not Plato, would have admitted. Possibly he was not fully alive to it. Nor was he embarrassed by the intrusion of the doctrine of 'flux' or 'becoming', as rendering impossible any clear conception of the individual or particular. The fact is, however, beyond dispute, that life would be largely robbed of its interest and variety if the mind of man dealt only with universals; the very joy and sap of existence would fail and the emotional life be severed at the root. Of this Roger Bacon (1214–94) was quite sure when he wrote: 'God has not created this world for the sake of the universal man, but for the sake of individual persons.'[38]

When a man's heart is tender toward the remembrance of his dead mother it is not of mothers-in-general, anybody's and everybody's mother, that he thinks; it is of *his* mother, incomparable; it is the one beloved voice that he hears; it is the one radiant smile that greets him;

> *That one face, far from vanish, rather grows,*
> *Or decomposes but to recompose.*[39]

Not to every man, as to Thomas Carlyle, is it granted to kindle to purely abstract notions, however exalted they may be; notions sometimes as featureless as his naked Duke addressing a naked House of Lords. Universals need to be clothed upon before they deeply move the majority of men —and then they have become *particulars*. Even the universals that we think do move us often turn out on closer inspection to be particulars in disguise. Helen of Troy, for example, has become a type, a kind of universal. Even in the time of Æschylus she was becoming a symbol, but of bitter things;

> *a vengeance and a token*
> *Of the unfaith to bread broken*
> *And the hearth of God betrayed.*[40]

But time has dealt gently with her and allowed her beauty to make large atonement for her sin. She is still a universal, a symbol, but of a fairer order; she is the *Woman of Man's Desiring*. As Walter Pater wrote of *La Giaconda*, she is 'expressive of what in the ways of a thousand years men had come to desire'.[41] Poets have sung her praises; artists have tried to portray her; and every true lover in his ecstatic moments has cried with Kit Marlowe's *Faust*,

> *all is dross that is not Helena.*

Theseus, in *A Midsummer Night's Dream*, knew these lovers:
> *the lover*
> *Sees Helen's beauty in a brow of Egypt.*[42]

Helen! the Universal!—and yet, not Helen!

Was Thomas Nashe trying to dislodge her from her already ancient pedestal when he wrote

> *Queens have died young and fair;*
> *Dust hath closed Helen's eye?* [43]

Men will not believe it while a true lover lives. Over three hundred years later Rupert Brooke attempted to sacrifice her on the altar of his destructive imagination and wrote his two sonnets to her and Menelaus. In spite of her betrayal of him, and even as he burned to slay her, Menelaus

> *Flung the sword away,*
> *And kissed her feet, and knelt before her there,*
> *The perfect Knight before the perfect Queen.*

Then the poet hurls at us his pitiless contrast, telling how, as years passed, Helen became

> *a scold,*
> *Haggard with virtue. Menelaus bold*
> *Waxed garrulous, and sacked a hundred Troys*
> *'Twixt noon and supper. And her golden voice*
> *Got shrill as he grew deafer. And both were old.* [44]

As we read, the Universal Helen of Man's Desiring flickers wraithlike, but only for a moment. She is too secure for Rupert Brooke's undoing.

To Walter de la Mare this 'strange, fabled face' is the image of Despair, because she is the Unattainable of men's dreams:

> *The voyagers of the world with sail and heavy oar*
> *Have sought thy shrine.*
> *Beauty inexorable hath lured them on.*
>
> *. . . . in tissue of gold*
> *Thine apparition gathers in the air—*
> *Nay, but the seas are deep, and the round world old,*
> *And thou art named Despair.* [45]

Perhaps! But in every new-born lover's life she is recreated from the ashes of some forerunner's hopelessness.

Why, one asks, this persistence of the Universal? Partly, perhaps, because we can expend our emotions upon these tenuous creations without betraying the secret of the concrete particulars that inspire them.

Helen of Troy is, after all, only the lover's clothes-pole; a mellifluous name that lends its beauty and its halo of romance to his rhapsody. His 'particular' Helen may be Betsy Snooks, who never heard of Menelaus, Paris or Troy; who lives in a little house in the next street: works in a milliner's shop in the daytime and goes with him to the 'flicks' at night. Helen's, indeed, was

> *the face that launched a thousand ships,*
> *And burnt the topless towers of Ilium,*[46]

but that was far away and long ago. It is Betsy's kiss, real or imagined, that has, in a few burning, golden moments, made him immortal. Universals are the counters of men's logic and the lay figures of their dreams, and they only come to life when transformed into their apposite particulars. John Davies depopulates and impoverishes the human mind when he makes it the habitation of universals rather than particulars. It is in universals that philosophers think; it is in particulars that men remember, because it is particulars that stir the crucibles of our lives.

More obvious is the Soul's independence of Time, for,

> *She is sent as soone to China as to Spaine,*
> *And thence returns, as soon as she is sent.*

Our poet goes on to assert the soul's creation as a direct act of God, citing, of course, the story in the Book of Genesis, and seeking to strengthen his case by the analogy of Minerva springing full-born from the cloven head of Jupiter:

> *So our true Jove, without a mother's ay'd,*
> *Doth daily millions of Minervas breed.*

We wince a little and let it pass.

Having glanced at such uncongenial and unorthodox theories as Transmigration and the generation of the Soul by human parents, Davies rejects them and states the case for Divine Creation. He draws a clear and pertinent distinction between Creation and Generation, ascribing the former to God alone. Generation is the production of like from like. He dismisses the possibility of that in the case of souls, on the ground that no like stuff exists upon which the generating power can work. By Creation he means production from Nothing. Over against the dictum of Lucretius and the Epicureans, *nil posse creari de nilo*,[47] he posits the agency of God as the sole exception, on the then generally unquestioned interpretation of the Hebrew cosmogony. It is interesting to observe how this useful distinction between Creation on the one hand and Generation or Emanation on the other, is used by a thinker so modern and refreshing as Nicholas Berdyaev. In *The Destiny of Man* he writes:

Creation is different in principle from generation and emanation. In emanation particles of matter radiate from a centre and are separated off. Nor is creation a re-distribution of force and energy, as evolution is. So far from being identical with evolution, creation is the very opposite of it. *In evolution nothing new is made, but the old is redistributed.* Evolution is *necessity*, creation is *freedom*. Creation is the greatest mystery of life, the mystery of the appearance of something new that had never existed before and is not deduced from, or generated by, anything. Creativeness presupposes non-being, μὴ ὄν (and not οὐκ ὄν) which is the source of the primeval, pre-cosmic, pre-existent freedom in man.... *Out of being, out of something that exists, it is impossible to create that which is absolutely new.* ... Creativeness means breaking through from non-being, from freedom, to the world of being. The mystery of creativeness is revealed in the Biblical myth of the Creation. God created the world out of nothing, i.e., freely and out of freedom. The world was not an emanation from God, it was not evolved or born from Him, but created, i.e., it was absolutely new, it was something that had never been before.[48] [Italics are mine.]

Thus Berdyaev deals with those conditions which are

prior to any evolutionary process or any product of human genius, ingenuity or skill; the field of provision or origin of the wherewithal that alone can give any meaning to the words *generate* and *evolve*. His statement is challenging. This *Non-being*, which elsewhere he calls *the Meonic* (μὴ ὄν), he regards as an actual entity, the sole 'material' (but it is not *material*) out of which God brought and still brings into being whatever is *wholly new*. When he says that 'creativeness means breaking through from non-being', the mind instinctively asks what it is that 'breaks through'. Does not *non-being* imply non-existence, and can the non-existent 'break through'? To regard μὴ ὄν as an entity or an existent does not dispel the mystery of pre-being, a condition probably for ever unrealizable by intelligence. Can *explanation* ever be achieved by exchanging a vernacular, descriptive phrase for some Greek or Latin compound word that means much the same thing? It is often ingenious and helpful in this way to create a kind of shorthand for thought and conversation, and Berdyaev's insistence upon his *Meonic* as a state of perfect freedom is valuable: a state which knows no necessity such as Being becomes subject to from the moment of its inception. Creation is only possible where there is this perfect freedom; where there is any constraint, a measure of evolution or generation has already begun to operate.

That ideas so presented would have appealed to the philosophic mind of Davies one can hardly doubt; this presentation, indeed, he partly anticipates. The more elaborate statement of this modern thinker would have enabled him to strengthen and render still more attractive his case for the creation of souls as a direct act of God: *new souls, created out of nothing: out of the Meonic.*

The views of Davies on *Creation* must have gained the hearty approval of John Wesley. In his *Letter to the Reverend Mr. Law* (January 6th, 1756), he replies to the latter's contention that, a creation out of nothing is no better sense than a creation into nothing, as follows:

A creation *into nothing* is a contradiction in terms. Can you say a creation *out of nothing* is so? It is indeed tautology: since the single term *Creation* is equivalent with production out of nothing.

This, he maintains, is supported by the first verse of Genesis.[49]

Davies now turns back into familiar country whose soil is tensile to his tread. The best of Greek thinkers are with him, and, except the Bible, the men of his age and outlook knew no stronger or more gratifying support for their views.

> *Then is the* soule *from God: so* Pagans *say,*
> *Which saw by Nature's light her heavenly kind:*
> *Naming her kin to God, and God's bright ray,*
> *A citizen of Heaven to Earth confined.*

This was the Orphic view and it colours subsequent Greek thought. At the point, however, where Orphism regarded the descent of the soul from the realms of the blessed into the prison-house or tomb of the body as being the just consequence of pre-natal sin, later classical thought moved along other lines. Plato anatomizes the soul and regards only that part which has powers of reasoning as being of Divine origin. This part, as we have already seen, is precisely what John Davies means by the 'soul'; it is, *par excellence,* that part of a human being's spiritual make-up which, by the aid of Sense, Memory, and Imagination, *reasons,* and so differentiates him from the brute.

Davies proceeds to consider the question of the soul's corruption, with which he was more deeply concerned because of the incident of the Middle Temple. He sets forth the doctrine of Original Sin by stating that the soul

> *even in the wombe is sinfull, and accurst:*

but, although God is the creator of the soul, not for a moment must He be held in any way responsible for this sinfulness. Davies valiantly attempts to establish this irresponsibility upon an ethical basis and thus to adjust the competing claims of morality and contemporary orthodoxy. He is not very convincing to the modern mind, and having conducted us round the familiar theological mulberry bush he proceeds to examine other considerations that emerge, such as the Nature of the Union between Soul and Body; The Soul's Use of the Body's Powers; the Nature of the Soul's Intellectual Powers. According to the use which the Soul makes of its association with the Body, Davies distinguishes three kinds of human being:

> *Some, like plants, their veines doe onely fill;*
> *And some, like beasts, their senses' pleasure take;*
> *And some, like angels, doe contemplate still—*

familiar perennials in the Garden of Mortality!

This section of the poem concludes with an 'Acclamation' of Man, somewhat in the style of the Eighth Psalm, ending on a note of rapture before the Mystery of the Incarnation of the Son of God:

> *But it exceeds man's thought, to think how hie*
> *God hath raised Man, since God a man became;*
> *The angels doe admire this Misterie,*
> *And are astonisht when they view the same.*

So Davies draws nearer to the heart of the affirmation that has lured him on: THAT THE SOULE IS IMMORTAL AND CANNOT DIE.

In support of it he now adduces six reasons, all being found in the essential nature of the Soul itself, so that a man has to look within to find them.

> *Who so makes a mirror of his mind,*
> *And doth with patience view himselfe therein,*
> *His Soule's eternitie shall clearely find,*
> *Though th'other beauties be defac't with sin.*

There is, first, the general desire for knowledge. As this desire is presumably from God—(Davies seems to have forgotten Adam's sin at this point)—and as man's time on earth is too short for its satisfaction, it is reasonable to suppose that that

> *which is here begun,*
> *Hereafter must be perfected in heaven.*

Then follows a reason drawn from 'the motion of the soule', a phrase strange to modern ears. Davies stresses the 'divine discontent' of man; nothing here is finally satisfying, and the 'motion' of the soul is toward a satisfaction that can be found only in God. But God is Eternal Spirit, and can only be fully known and enjoyed in the realm of spirit. If, then, the soul aspires to this God, there must be a quality of eternity in its own spirituality, and he illustrates thus:

> *Water in conduit pipes, can rise no higher*
> *Than the wel-head, from whence it first doth spring:*
> *Then sith to eternall God shee doth aspire,*
> *Shee cannot be but an eternall thing.*

Further, in 'the better sort of spirits' there is a 'contempt of Death'. This could not be if the soul were persuaded that the death of the body means its own extinction, for

> *if we think of being turn'd to nought,*
> *A trembling horror in our soules we find.*

Men would not subject their bodies to risk, as in war and on the sea, unless

> *all Soules have a surviving thought;*
> *Therefore of death we thinke with quiet mind;*

and that 'quiet mind' stands to Davies as voucher for the soul's immortality.

His fourth reason is a surprising one. He postulates that in 'wicked soules' there is a fear of death, which is other than a fear of extinction,

> *For when Death's forme appears, she feareth not*
> *An utter quenching or extinguishment;*
> *She would be glad to meet with such a lot,*
> *That so she might all future ill prevent.*

It is fear of future punishment for sin, thought of as eternal, that is in this case the pointer to an after life, but this conclusion is arrived at by a mental process that is glaringly illicit. Davies is out to 'prove' the continued existence of the Soul. He says in effect: 'Wicked souls believe in future punishment: therefore there must be a future life in which that punishment is inflicted.' But clearly no soul could believe in future punishment unless it had entertained a *prior* belief in a future life. For a man of law, Davies trips badly. It is belief in a future life that makes belief in future punishment possible and not the reverse. Nor is our poet always as sophisticated as we expect a lawyer to be. At this point, for example, he asks

> *When was there ever cursèd atheist brought*
> *Unto the gibbet, but he did adore*
> *That blessed Power, which he had set at nought,*
> *Scorned and blasphemèd all his life before?*

Evidently an emphatic *Never* is expected, but the 'cursed atheists' thus engaged in adoration are few and far between.

After glancing at the 'Generall Desire of Immortalitie' as affording proof of it, Davies passes finally to 'the very Doubt and Disputation of Immortalitie'. He tries to show that the mere conception of Immortality by a human mind, even if it doubts or disbelieves, is evidence for its truth, for, on the analogy of

> *without Reason, none could Reason know,*

only that which is itself immortal is capable of entertaining the concept of Immortality; which is reminiscent of Samuel Johnson's historic retort:

> *Who drives fat oxen should himself be fat.* [50]

So he concludes:

> *Heaven waxeth old, and all the* spheres *above*
> *Shall one day faint, and their swift motion stay;*
> *And* Time *it selfe in time shall cease to move;*
> Onely the Soule survives, *and lives for aye.*

As Davies passes on to state and reply to current objections to this doctrine we note two points of special interest. To the objection that the dotage of old age indicates a soul waxing aged and brains grown 'sottish, dull, and cold': and that idiocy is the sign of a corrupt soul, he replies that the defect lies not in the soul but in the body and its organs of sense. These give a false report to the soul upon the nature of the objective world, but on that report, such as it is, the soul gives a logical and reasonable judgement: false in regard to objective reality: true in regard to the information which the soul possesses. To those who object that souls do not return

> *to bring us newes*
> *Of that strange world where they such wonders see,*

Davies replies that evidently their new abode is so greatly to their liking that nothing can induce them to leave it:

> *as Noah's pidgeon, which returned no more,*
> *Did shew, she footing found, for all the Flood;*
> *So when good soules, departed through Death's dore,*
> *Come not againe, it shewes their dwelling good,*

which may be a pretty conceit, but lacks convincing power. By analogous reasoning one would expect that departed souls whose dwelling place was not desirable *would* return. Perhaps Davies would account for their non-appearance by the restraint of their punishment.

So, at last, he arrives at a final 'Acclamation'. As he has thought and written, the conviction that his own soul is divine and immortal in its nature has been deepened. Apart from the dogma of the Fall and Hereditary Guilt of Man, and some slight references to the redeeming work of Christ, doctrine distinctively Christian finds little place in his pages, but one is conscious of it as his mental background. He is a religious man and a Christian Idealist philosopher, and whilst the modern mind challenges some of his conceptions and rebels, at times, against his presentation of arguments whose general relevance it admits, it is impossible to dismiss the whole poem as a negligible contribution to its subject. We read it and are impressed, and, finally, confess that, whilst all our questions have been neither raised nor adequately answered, our faith in the soul's immortality has been made more sure.

Whether his readers benefit or not by what Davies wrote, the impression is inescapable that he himself did; and probably about himself he was most deeply concerned. He is attempting, as he writes, to straighten out the twists and irregularities in his own thought and conduct. The follies of his life, with their unpleasant consequences, have forced him to think out his own worth to God, and he has expressed it in terms of the worth of every individual soul. It is thought with prayer at the heart of it. He is not that type of sinner who feels or professes to feel that he has sinned above all men and beyond hope of redemption. He has been a fool and acknowledges it ungrudgingly, but by virtue of his soul's divine and marvellous workmanship he is bold to seek divine grace and assistance in a wise and worthy fashioning of his life henceforward. His religion is based upon reasoned rather than emotional convictions. Such men, if they are poets, do not 'flame' like Richard Crashaw and Charles Wesley, but they have their place in the healthy, God-fearing ordering of a nation's life.

He emerges from his seclusion at last, fortified to meet the ills of life and resolute to serve his God in obedience to Duty's call. He is of the Immortals. He has passed beyond the alternating hope and fear of William Watson:

> *And ah, to know not, while with friends I sit,*
>   *And while the purple joy is passed about,*
> *Whether 'tis ampler day divinelier lit*
>   *Or homeless night without;*
>
> *And whether, stepping forth, my soul shall see*
>   *New prospects, or fall sheer—a blinded thing!*
> *There is, O Grave, thy hourly victory,*
>   *And there, O Death, thy sting.*[51]

Few are they who have never felt the urgency and poignancy of this questioning. But Davies is out in regions beyond these competing surmises and he would take you and me with him. How charitable his emancipated spirit! Listen!

> *O ignorant poor man! What does thou beare*
>   *Lockt up within the casket of thy brest?*
> *What jewels and what riches hast thou there!*
>   *What heavenly treasure in so weake a chest!*
>
> *Looke in thy* soule, *and thou shalt beauties find* . . .
>
> *Think of her worth, and think that God did meane,*
>   *This worthy mind should worthy things imbrace;*
> *Blot not her beauties with thy thoughts unclean,*
>   *Nor her dishonour with thy passions base.*
>
> *And when thou think'st of her eternitie,*
>   *Thinke not that* Death *against her nature is,*
> *Think it a birth; and when thou goest to die,*
>   *Sing like a swan, as if thou went'st to blisse.*

With that stanza in our ears we close the book and wonder why the dust of years lies so thickly upon its covers. It is not because of unfavourable judgement by contemporary or later readers and critics, for we note, without surprise, with what respect they treat him, both as philosopher and poet. That John Wesley thought very highly of his work we have already noted. Under date, Monday, 21st April, 1760, he wrote: 'In riding to Rosmead I read Sir John Davis's [sic] *Historical Relations concerning Ireland.*' There follows a brief outline of the book, penned with evident appreciation of its author's sympathetic and discerning attitude toward the Irish people in general. When, in 1745, Wesley compiled a list of books to guide his preachers in their reading, the only English poets included were Spenser, Milton, and—Sir John Davies.[52] In his anthology, *A Collection of Moral and Sacred Poems*, Wesley included the whole of the forty-five introductory stanzas of *Nosce Teipsum*, bearing the sub-title *Of Humane Knowledge*, and also the nine stanzas, 'An Acclamation', with which the poem ends. The latter he also printed in his *Arminian Magazine* for 1788. Parts of Wesley's sermon on 'The Good Steward' suggest that he had recently re-read *Nosce Teipsum* from which he quotes, not quite accurately,

a dying sparkle in a cloudy place,

and

looks through the windows of the eye and ear.[53]

Davies may have his day again in some select circle of appreciative readers. He writes easily and his rhythms have natural stresses. Nothing is forced, not even his rhymes. Rarely is there any fumbling for a word and about many there is an air of inevitability. The writing of good didactic verse is a rare and difficult accomplishment, but Davies possesses it and makes his meaning crystal clear. He is never dull nor is his poem a mere academic exercise. We may smile today at some of his 'arguments' and similes, but always he holds our attention and directs the stream of our thought. At the end we feel very tender toward him. He has not demonstrated the undemonstrable: being reasonable people we have not expected that; but he has *fortified the probable* and we are grateful.

Poetic inspiration was for Davies incidental rather than constitutional and he did not repeat his performance. He had his moment on the Mount of Vision and came down, never to find his way back. That was part of the price which he paid for the possession of distinguished administrative talents; the exactions of public life and office barred the way of his return. There must have been moments when he looked back wistfully to that land of lost delights, that magic kingdom of Poesy. There he might have lived out his happy days and travelled far, for his work was received with instant acclamation. We are told that 'ye first essay of his pen was so well relisht yt ye queen (Elizabeth) encouraged him in his studdys, promising him preferment and had him sworn her servant in ordinary'.

Scholar though Davies was, he wrote a poem for the plain man, and much in it may serve as an admirable directive and corrective in life. Perhaps, after all our more recondite searchings, our more subtle conclusions and our modern psychology, it is the simpler, plainer ideas and distinctions of John Davies that have greater determining effect upon our lives. The advice which John Wesley gave to a friend in December 1762 might well serve to introduce this poem to the average man, unskilled in dialectics:

Hold fast whereunto you have attained, and do not *reason* about it. Do not concern yourself whether it should be called by this or another name. It is right as far as it goes. And whatsoever is yet lacking, God is able and willing to supply.[54]

As we review the poem in a meditative moment we recall one of John Davies's great contemporaries. John Donne was born when Davies was four years old and he outlived him by five years. Both had survived the buffetings of a perverse and tempestuous youth, emerging stronger and clearer-eyed, to come at length, the one almost to the dignity of Lord Chief Justice and the other to the Deanery of St. Paul's. That they should not have met is almost inconceivable, and in thought and in ways of penitence, amendment, and spiritual conviction they were at one. We behold them, in their more mature years, bowed in reverence before the wonder and beauty of their immortal souls and we say our Farewell with the golden accents of Donne, speaking for both, ringing in our ears:

Through the ragged apparell of the afflictions of this life; through the scarres and wounds, and palenesse, and morphews of sin, and corruption, we can look upon the soul it self, and there see that incorruptible beauty, that *white* and *red*, which the *innocency* and the *blood* of Christ hath given it, and we are mad for love of this soul, and ready to doe any act of danger, in the ways of persecution, any act of diminution of our selves in the ways of humiliation, *to stand at her doore*, and *pray*, and *begge*, that *she would be reconciled to God*.[55]

God gave me the light of Nature when I quickned in my mothers wombe by receiving a reasonable soule; and God gave me the light of faith, when I quickned in my second mothers womb, the Church, by receiving my baptisme; but in my third day, when my mortality shall put on immortality, he shall give me the light of glory, by which I shall see himself.[56]

V

A Cynic among Sectaries

Henry More—1614–87

THE LONELY voyager on the multitudinous and stormy seas of post-Reformation theological controversy will come in some auspicious hour to a fair haven of repose: the haunt of a little group of divines, dwelling within their own 'olive grove of Academe' the 'Cambridge Platonists': who, if he be spiritually and intellectually of their company, will welcome him with the grave courtesy of 'the two shining men' who greeted Christian and Hopeful as they emerged from the waters of Jordan: 'We are ministering spirits, sent forth to minister to them who shall be heirs of salvation.' They were some seven in number; born, with one exception, in the second decade of the seventeenth century; owning Cambridge as their common nursing mother; bred in the same theological climate and exposed to the same political and religious influences. They were also men of piety and erudition, for whom a valid religious faith must have an intellectual foundation. Like Clement of Alexandria and Origen, their philosophical outlook was essentially Platonist. In one of those oracular utterances on which, one suspects, he prided himself considerably, Emerson declared: 'There are not in the world at any one time more than a dozen persons who read and understand Plato.' Presumably this meant, at the time of writing, Ralph Waldo Emerson and eleven others, including, possibly, a certain Benjamin Jowett, of Balliol College, in Oxford. In the mid-seventeenth century it would have meant, after Cambridge had received its due, that only some half-dozen from the rest of mankind could have qualified for the distinction, for the members of this group were students and disciples of Plato to a man. They examined Christian doctrine in the light of the Idealist philosophy and accepted it with heart and mind. *Qualis philosophus talis theologus.* From the brawls of Laudian High Churchmen, Presbyterians, Independents, and Puritan sectaries they stood calmly and, it must be admitted, somewhat superciliously aloof. Perhaps a measure of this attitude is inevitable to the Platonist as he looks abroad and observes many of the occasions of human discord and how men

> *lost in stormy visions, keep*
> *With phantoms an unprofitable strife,*
> *And in mad trance, strike with [their] spirit's knife*
> *Invulnerable nothings.*[1]

As he marks the fatuous discussions and childish judgements of so many of his fellow mortals and how true it frequently is that

> *the meaning doesn't matter*
> *If its only idle chatter*
> *Of a transcendental kind,*[2]

—nor is it always 'transcendental'—can a Platonist wholly avoid it? The temptation to regard certain of these people as amusing and yet rather irritating *homunculi* is, on occasion, difficult to resist, but if he is, as he ought to be, a genuine humanitarian, he will make a valiant effort so to do. Whilst ecclesiastics of various schools wrangled about such puerile matters as infallibilities, postures, vestments, and validities, the Cambridge men were concerned to affirm the reality of God and the Soul of Man against the advance guard of a sceptical, materialistic, anti-Scholastic philosophy, represented by Thomas Hobbes, and proclaiming that Substance alone has reality. Apparently these Churchmen failed entirely to perceive that, in so far as this type of Thought should prevail, the subjects of their own disputings would appear still more puerile and more than ever irrelevant to the life and well-being of man, and the Christian Religion itself become an anachronism.

The 'Cambridge Platonists' were also known as 'Latitude Men' or 'Latitudinarians', and Bishop Burnet, who was their contemporary, but of a generation later, refers to them, in his *History of His Own Times*, in terms of warm commendation, holding that, because of the idleness, love of luxury and neglect of duty on the part of many bishops and clergy, 'the credit of the Church had been quite extinct'[3] but for them. W. R. Sorley reminds us that

they appeared when the High Church system of Laud was in the ascendant; they flourished under the rule of the Presbyterians and of the Independents; and the Restoration scarcely disturbed them. *They did not take sides with any existing parties*. . . . Their doctrine was equally removed from Calvinism and High Churchism. They avoided the subtleties of the prevailing theologies, opposed credulity and enthusiasm (or the claim to private inspiration), held that true religion must harmonize with rational truth and laid stress on the moral and spiritual factors in religion.[4]

Benjamin Whichcote, whom some regard as the originator of the group, expressed the convictions of them all when he said: 'there is no genuine and proper effect of religion where the mind of man is not composed, sedate and calm'.[5] Such a mind they cultivated with marked success in a peculiarly tempestuous age. They were such men as confer honour and dignity upon the Church of England, or any Christian communion to which they happen to belong; who have their counterparts in every generation, and who go far to atone for the discredit cast upon the Christian Church by men of meaner, childish mind and limited outlook.

None of their number attained to greater distinction than Henry More. He was born at Grantham in 1614, his father being 'a gentleman of fair estate and fortune', a Calvinist in his theology but a non-Puritan in his churchmanship. At fourteen Henry went to Eton and three years later to Christ's College, Cambridge, where for seven months he was a junior contemporary of John Milton. Upon graduating in 1639 he took holy orders, though it is almost certain that he never preached a sermon in his life. At the same time he was elected a fellow of his college and so continued to his death in 1687. He was innocent of such ambitions as inspire ordinary people and would have agreed heartily with the words of his contemporary, Sir Thomas Browne:

Be substantially great in thyself, and more than thou appearest unto others. . . . Hang early plummets upon the heels of Pride, and let Ambition have but an Epicycle and narrow circuit in thee. . . . If thou must needs rule, be Zeno's king, and enjoy that Empire which every man gives himself.[6]

This More did. He loved beauty and comfort, though not to excess, and his book-lined study in Christ's College was Paradise on earth to him. His friends knew him as a happy man, who delighted in music and Nature, and to whom the visible world was the Garment of the Spirit of God. He declined the Mastership of his College and offers of Church preferment left him cold; all he desired was the quiet, occupied, happy life of a fellow. Friends, however, were ambitious on his behalf, and on one occasion he was almost persuaded to gratify them by going to Whitehall to kiss the royal hand. When he understood that this was the ceremonial act of acceptance of a bishopric he refused to go farther and the scheme came to nought. 'I have measured myself,' he once said, 'and know what I can do and what I ought to do, and I do it'—truly a valiant response to the ancient challenge γνῶθι σεαυτόν. Such a man cannot be far from the Kingdom of God.

Mr. Basil Willey, in his *Seventeenth-century Background*, admirably describes More as a man of deep religious convictions:

With Henry More ... the existence of the spiritual world was the first of certainties, and most of his works are designed to prove its reality....
With him the reality of 'spirit' was more than an intellectual conviction, it was an experience. As with Coleridge, a sense of the divine presence interpenetrating all things seems to have been inborn in him, and he was conscious of it very early in his life. He speaks of 'that exceeding hail and entire sense of God, which nature herself had planted deeply in me', and declares that his mind 'was enlightened with a sense of the noblest theories in the morning of his days'.[7]

Plato, Plotinus, and their school influenced him profoundly, as also did Edmund Spenser, and, guided by them, he arrived at the conviction that self-will must be utterly suppressed if the Divine Will is wholly to prevail in a man's life. His early and passionate desire for knowledge was gradually modified as this conviction grew, and his reliance upon reason and love of dialectic yielded, in his later years, to a complex, diffuse mysticism which professed to find in Hebrew and Early Christian Prophecy and Apocalyptic the master key to all knowledge. Plato decreased and the Book of Daniel, that scapegoat of religious credulity, increased. His distrust of Philosophy, as capable of giving any other than a 'dusty answer' to the soul that is 'hot for certainties in this our life', is probably shared by most thoughtful persons, but when such a man as More believes that he has found the key to all wisdom and to all knowledge in writers of apocalyptic, who would themselves, probably, have been the first to protest astonishment, one can only exclaim: 'The pity of it! O! the pity of it!' There was, however, a greater measure of reason in More's later mystical intuitions than he was willing to admit, but all the same, as the later years of his life sped on, it was sorrowfully true of him,

never glad, confident morning again![8]

We are concerned only with the More wearing 'the beauty of the morning', the man who at the age of twenty-eight published a volume of poems with the forbidding title, *Psychodia Platonica, or a Platonicall Song of the Soul*, with various sub-titles. The book contains four long poems but only a part of the first will claim our attention. Its title is *The Argument of Psychozoia, Or, the Life of the Soul.* In commercial matters More was clearly a poor psychologist and could have learned something about the art of salesmanship from the meanest shopkeeper in Cambridge. In a wholly other connexion, Julian Huxley says:

You do not—in the long run at least—make a thing more important by giving it an imposing title; you only give it a false exclusiveness.[9]

There is natural wisdom in putting goods in an attractive wrapper. Our Christmas gifts, however small and inexpensive in themselves, gain sentimental value and charm by being presented in bright, 'Christmassy' paper. But by his title-wrapper More seems to say to the average man, 'What I have written is not for you,' which is a pity, for he has much which the reader of good literature would enjoy. The author seems eventually to have realized this, for in a later edition he made his title-page a little, but only a very little, more attractive by substituting English for his bastard Greek. Perhaps he looked at his book somewhat as Juliet looked at Romeo:

> *'Tis but thy name that is my enemy!*
> *O, be some other name!—*

which is possible in a second edition of a book; but there are no second editions of the world's Romeos—or at any rate the Juliets think not. When, however, she continues,

> *What's in a name! that which we call a rose*
> *By any other name would smell as sweet,*[10]

we demur. The name, in the case of a rose, may matter little (though names may be euphonious or otherwise), because in one exuberant moment it flaunts its beauty and

[105]

yields up its perfume. Not so with a book! Its name may imprison its loveliness and stifle its fragrance, as More's title must have done for many a questing spirit, presenting a barrier too discouraging for most people even to attempt to over-ride.

His writings were never popular and one may safely predict that they never will be, but to be a 'best seller' is no criterion of literary excellence or immortality. One feels that, rightly or wrongly, More would have disdained literary popularity as others have done. Pistol, when on sentry duty, was suddenly confronted by King Henry the Fifth, whom he failed to recognize and challenged. Then he commenced a conversation:

> *Discuss unto me; art thou officer?*
> *Or art thou* base, common, *and* popular?

Whether or not he was being cynical, Pistol lumped the three attributes together as if any one implied the other two. The King responded,

> *I am a gentleman of a company.*[11]

There you are, Pistol! Make what you like of that. Even so, to one eager to spur him on to popularity, might More have responded: 'I am a gentleman of a company'; and a select and distinguished company it was, especially if we pay homage to Emerson's pontifical pronouncement. Certainly 'low ambition and the thirst of praise' were distasteful to More and obviously he shrank from, if he did not positively fear, that popularity which may be the thief of a man's time and a dead weight upon the independence of his spirit. Leaders of men like John Wesley have been acutely aware of this and that distinguished man warned his preachers in grave and sane words which, *mutatis mutandis*, have general pertinence for gifted men everywhere who hear the siren call of a presumptive popularity.[12]

How [he asks in his peremptory way] shall we avoid popularity? We mean such esteem or love from the people as is not for the glory of God.

1. Earnestly pray for a piercing sense of the danger and the sinfulness of it.
2. Take care how you ingratiate yourself with any people by slackness of discipline. [If you have literary gifts, don't *write down* to the uncritical mob or you may become a mere 'hack.']
3. Warn the people among whom you are most, of esteeming or loving you too much. [Lest they lose their power of independent judgement and become merely your echo.]
4. Converse sparingly with those who are particularly fond of you. [Lest their flattery blind your eyes, stop your ears and dull your understanding.][1]

Wesley always followed his own advice. In April 1745, when, according to his *Journal*, 'the rich and great' of Newcastle were flocking to hear him, so that often the room would not hold them, and 'it is almost *fashionable* to speak well of us', he departed in haste and wrote: 'It was time for me to give them the ground at Newcastle and *to fly for my life*. I grew more and more honourable every day.'[13]

A man after More's own heart, in more respects than one! We know that Wesley held the Cambridge men in high regard. Whilst Wesley feared popularity as an ever-threatening danger, with More it never threatened because he never allowed it the opportunity. Probably he held with Plutarch that

To please the many is to displease the wise,[14]

but in avoiding the Scylla of Popularity such a man must navigate his course carefully or he may be drawn into the Charybdis of Snobbery. It can hardly be said that he wholly escaped that whirlpool or looked as kindly as he might have done upon mankind in the mass. Did he ever note how his beloved Plato ended one of his letters to Dion of Syracuse?

And, Dion, remember also that you are held by some to be unduly lacking in affability; forget not, therefore, that successful action is dependent upon pleasing people, whereas Snobbery ($αὐθάδεια$) is next-door neighbour to Isolation. (To a desert. $ἐρημίᾳ$). Good luck to you![15]

[1] The words in brackets are the writer's.

More himself provides us with a kind of guide-book for our literary journey. '*Psychozoia*' first appeared in 1642, and in later years, when his mental life had undergone that puzzling reorientation to which reference has been made, he tells us that about the beginning of the year 1640 he was moved to write these poems by 'some Heavenly Impulse of Mind', and that he did it 'with no other Design, than that it should remain by me, a private record of the Sensations and Experiences of my own Soul'. In old age he made further reference to it as 'rather obscure, especially that part written in a style harsh and unpolished (though it was otherwise vivid enough)'. He then thought it 'difficult for anyone that chanced upon it to understand what the poet wished; yet I often considered burning it myself, lest it should fall into the hands of others. Therefore it lay in my desk suppressed for some time.' Finally, having shown it to 'certain learned and godly men', it was published, to the exceeding comfort of some odds and ends of posterity. One wonders if he was moved at all by the impish spirit of Byron:

> *I'll publish, right or wrong;*
> *Fools are my theme, let satire be my song,*[16]

for satire is there in delicious abundance as we shall see.

There is further and more valuable guidance in the explanatory preface which More issued with his book. It is, indeed, almost indispensable for an intelligent reading of what follows.

It is idle to pretend that his poetry is for *Everyman*. Even the most expert reader will not address himself to it with such ease as, let us say, he will sample a volume of poetry by Rupert Brooke or W. H. Davies. *Psychozoia* is in three books and in the first and the early part of the second the author expounds his metaphysical mysticism in allegorical form, and in such terms and with such strange nomenclature as would have beguiled the spirit of William Blake: a curious, often harsh compound of the whimsical and the erudite: hybrid monstrosities of Greek and Hebrew origin. Occasionally he coins a word which is a combination of roots from both languages. Did his better known contemporary, Samuel Butler, have *Psychozoia* in mind when, in *Hudibras*, he described the 'metaphysical sectarian'?

> *his speech in loftiness of sound was rich;*
> *A Babylonish dialect, which learned pedants much affect;*
> *It was a party-coloured dress of patched and piebald languages;*
> *'Twas English cut on Greek and Latin,*
> *Like fustian heretofore on sattin.*[17]

To some people the early stanzas will prove a dry, dusty terrain, studded with bizarre and grotesque features, and to one unwilling to concentrate and persevere the journey is likely to be one of increasing boredom, perplexity, and mental fatigue. Probably, like Bunyan's Pliable, he will fall into a Slough of Despond, and on emerging return to the place whence he came, to seek other company than Henry More's; which is to be regretted. But, by being content to travel slowly at first, those conscientious souls who scorn the art of even judicious skipping, will overcome the difficulties of More's style and the intricacy of his matter, and presently find themselves reading with keen enjoyment and many a chuckle. Very much will depend upon the reader's interest in the landscape. If he should be one of those rare individuals to whom philosophical mysticism of any kind makes a strong appeal, the journey will be one of ever-growing fascination and he will clear the obstacles with the skill of a trained mental and spiritual athlete.

The people whom we meet in the early stages of our journey are personalized abstractions, most of whom have forbidding names. Everywhere we are conscious of the ghostly presences of Plato, Plotinus, and their later disciples. More is working out, in allegorical form, a theory of a mystical neo-Platonic Triad, corresponding to the Christian Doctrine of the Trinity. These abstractions have multiple names, each corresponding to some inherent quality or function, and from the welter of More's mysticism there emerges at length one clear, attractive figure, in whom later interest centres: *Psyche* or *Uranora,* the latter descriptive name being a compound of the ordinary Greek word for Sky or Heaven, οὐρανός, and אוֹר, the common Hebrew word for Light: *Uranora,* the *Light,* or *Beauty of Heaven.* She is the third person of this metaphysical Triad, corresponding to the Holy Spirit, and is the daughter of the *All-Father,* the first person. From her marriage with the second person, *Æon* (Eternity or Being), spring all the souls of men, and through her they participate in the Divine Life. More presents her in various aspects; amongst others, she is the principle of physical life as it acts upon matter and produces consciousness and form.

More sees the Universe in all its aspects, material and immaterial, as the Robe of Uranora, and this gives ample scope for his descriptive powers. Here are passages of unusual beauty that exhibit More the poet as distinct from More the philosopher. For example, he sees dawn break over the world and night presently creep on and writes:

> *There you may see the eyelids of the Morn*
> *With lofty silver arch displayed in the East,*
> *And in the midst the burnished gold doth burn;*
> *A lucid, purple mantle in the West*
> *Doth close the day, and hap the Sun at rest.*

He refers to God as

> *deeply covered o'er*
> *With unseen light. No might imaginable*
> *May reach that vast profundity.*

Having drawn our attention to the sunset sky, where

> *light and changing tinctures deck this goodly veil,*

he continues:

But 'mongst these glaring, glittering rows of light,
And flaming Circles, and the grizzly gray,
And crudled [curdled] clouds, with silver tippings dight,
And many other deckings wondrous gay,
As Iris [rainbow] and the Halo [of sun or moon], there doth play
Still-paced Euphrona [Night] in her Conique [cone-like] tire;
By stealth her steeple-cap she doth assay
To whelm on the earth.

The last three lines reveal More as a disciple of the New Astronomy, as also the following, wherein his mood about Night has changed:

> *those far shining Rounds in open skies:*
> *Their course the best Astronomer might well dismay.*

These danced about [planets]; but some I did espy
That steady stood, 'mongst which there shined one,
More fairly shineth not the world's great eye,
Which from his plenteous store unto the Moon
Kindly imparteth light, that when he's gone,
She might supply his place, and well abate
The irksome ugliness of that foul drone,
Sad, heavy Night. . . .

—a harsh rescinding of the lovely Greek name which he so recently gave to her—*Euphrona*, the *Kindly Season*!

We leave now these phantoms of gossamer and ichor in their metaphysical cloud-land and tread solid earth again. Here live men and women who are the offspring of Psyche and Æon, their souls divinely created. They are presented to us as gravely concerned about their destiny in the Hereafter, which More declares to be determined by their attitude to God in this earthly stage of being. Therefore he urges them to seek God without delay, through their own intuitions and the Christian revelation, and to mistrust a religion of simple Naturalism:

Therefore thy God seek out, and leave Nature behind.

Having sketched the conditions of the after-life of the ungodly as he conceives them, he rises to some of his most inspired lines to declare,

> *But souls that of His own good life partake*
> *He loves as His own self; dear as His eye*
> *They are to Him: He'll never them forsake:*
> *When they shall die then God Himself shall die.*
> *They live, they live in blest Eternity.*

—words that so impressed Emerson that he quoted them as preface to his essay on *The Over-Soul*.

More appropriately calls this country of souls *Psychania*. It is sub-divided into two kingdoms and these again into provinces, each under its ruler. The 'souls' are distributed throughout these provinces, each according to its nature, the provinces being the various 'climates' in which souls exist. He introduces us to a part of Psychania named *Beirah*, בער = brutishness, stupidity, where dwell souls that are in slavery to Self and the unregenerate, animal desires of man. Should these souls gain even a little wisdom they will seek to escape from this brutish land to *Theoprepia*, the country of god-like souls, that are in possession of their spiritual faculties and the enjoyment of their privileges as God-created beings.

At this point in the poem we are introduced to Mnemon (μνήμων, remembering), whose name is taken straight from Spenser's *Faerie Queene*. He is an embodiment of mystical religion: a kind of gathered remembrance of More's own experiences and moods, and we need always to bear in mind that he is the mouthpiece of More's own convictions; that More himself speaks in every word of this, his understudy. Physically the two were wholly unlike, for More describes him thus:

> Old Mnemon's head and beard were hoary white,
> But yet a cheerful countenance he had;
> His vigorous eyes did shine like starres bright,
> And in good decent frieze he was yclad,
> As blithe and buxom as was any lad
> Of one and twenty, clothed in forest green;
> Both blithe he was, and eke of counsel sad;
> Like winter-morn bedight with snow and rime
> And sunny rays, so did his goodly Eldship shine.

This engaging old gentleman, with his wide experience of men and things and his detached, observant and cynically humorous attitude to life, takes up the story and recounts some of his adventures.

On one occasion, he tells us, when he was much younger, he was travelling in a part of Beirah named *Psittacusa*: the *Land of Parrots*. Let us notice, at this point, that More gives bird names to many of the characters that people his story, somewhat in the style of Chaucer in his *Parlement of Foules*, but whereas Chaucer actually turns his people into birds, More attempts no such metamorphosis; his characters remain human beings, but they strut and undulate with such marked avian absurdities that he baptizes them anew into the kingdom of the fowls. His mordant irony would have delighted that master of the ironic art, the author of *Penguin Island*, M. Anatole France. Taking birds instead of beasts, More works out the idea of Sir John Hayward:

As every kind of beast is principally inclined to one sensuality more than to another, so man transformeth himself into that beast to whose sensuality he principally declines.[18]

This part of the poem is a kind of running commentary on the ecclesiastical world of More's day and some of the people in it, the latter being easily identifiable by the student of the seventeenth century. For the general reader today they are types that still survive and crop up in successive generations. Perhaps they have their uses to usward as God's mentors, so that, as we regard them we say: 'There, but for the grace of God, go I.' The historian may say: 'Ah! This is Archbishop Laud. That is a divine of the Westminster Assembly', but, as we read, the whole historical pageant fades away and we recognize men whom we met or heard of only a few days ago. More is concerned with the outward expressions of Religion as throwing light upon its inward reality, or non-reality; with forms and ceremonies; with professions of faith and the Seat of Authority in Religion. The people whom we meet in his allegory have some kind of 'form' without the 'power' of Godliness. His was an age of warring sectaries.[19] On the one hand there was the extreme 'High Churchman'—that is, of the Laudian type. His modern successor of that ilk lay two hundred years deep in the womb of time. At the other extreme was a motley crowd of Puritan sectaries, while the Presbyterians and Independents trod a middle way. The attitude of More and his fellow Platonists was, as we have seen, one of slightly cynical aloofness. The presence of any one of these sectaries stimulated his sympathies with the others. Let us bear in mind that he was an ordained minister of the Church of England and walked with intelligence in a middle way: neither Puritan nor wholly anti-Puritan: neither ritualist nor wholly anti-ritualist. From this position he looked at the antics and listened to the jargon of the extremists, all of whom presented him with opportunities of exercising his gift of satire and of these he generously availed himself; satire for the most part lost upon its victims, close-mailed as they were in the armour of their conceit, but affording intense delight to men whose God is 'the Lord, the Creator of the ends of the Earth', and not the custodian deity of the local parish pump.

We prepare ourselves, then, to meet some of these 'bird' types of the ecclesiastical, as distinct from the religious, world, and More, under the pseudonym of Mnemon, is our guide.

He tells us how, travelling on horseback through *Psittacusa* (Parrot Land), he was overtaken and accosted by one of its inhabitants, a cleric, Don Psittaco—the Reverend Mr. Parrot, let us say—a representative of the extreme Puritan faction. His appearance, mannerisms and discourse move Mnemon to laughter which he tries, in politeness, to repress, but in vain.

> *His concave nose, great head and grave aspect,*
> *Affected tone, words without inward sense,*
> *My inly tickled spright* [spirit] *made me detect* [be detected]
> *By outward laughter; but by best pretence*
> *I purged myself, and gave due reverence.*

The perfect parrot! Moving us to laughter as a bird! To more riotous laughter as a man!

> *I gave the talk to him, which pleased him well,*

says Mnemon, but it was all 'words without inward sense'; a medley of sounds on Biblical Criticism, Scripture Commentaries, and the 'brilliant learning' that was supposed to be a distinguishing mark of the seventeenth century. Again Mnemon breaks into silent but irrepressible laughter:

> *I, alas! though unto him unseen,*
> *Did flow with tears, as if that onyons keen*
> *Had pierced mine eyen.*

He might have been boon companion to Shakespeare's Jacques, meeting Touchstone in the forest:

> *A fool, a fool! I met a fool i'th' forest,*
> *A motley fool. . . .*

> *When I did hear*
> *The motley fool thus moral on the time,*
> *My lungs began to crow like chanticleer,*
> *That fools should be so deep contemplative;*
> *And I did laugh sans intermission*
> *An hour by his dial.*[20]

Such laughter cleanses the human spirit of its unhealthy humours. Recall the 'ruffianly English soldier' in the Epilogue of G. B. Shaw's *Saint Joan*, who was having his annual day's holiday from Hell. He appears singing,

> *Rum tum trumpledum,*
> *Bacon fat and rumpledum,*
> *Old saint mumpledum,*
> *Pull his tail and stumpledum,*
> *O my Ma—ry Ann!*

The censure of the scornful only sends his already high spirits up a notch or two and he explains:

We made it up ourselves as we marched. We were not gentlefolk and troubadours. Music straight out of the heart of the people, as you might say.... It don't mean anything, you know; but it keeps you marching.

Shaw's common soldier had this advantage over Don Psittaco: he *knew* that his words were without sense, and so he and his companions, and even his critics if they were so minded, could laugh uproariously together without fear of hurting each others' feelings: and when men laugh together at their own absurdities they contribute to the peace of the world and the general contentment of mankind. It was Mnemon alone who laughed at the absurdities of Don Psittaco, but all silently and stealthily, or the peace of the immediate world might have been broken. So we put More, the real Mnemon, a little higher on the pedestal of human excellence, for is it not written in the Book of *Sartor Resartus*, after Teufelsdröckh had delivered himself of the historic and only known laugh of his life, that 'no man who has once heartily and wholly laughed can be altogether irreclaimably bad'?[21]

The situation is fortunately relieved at this moment by the appearance of a swaggering young jackanapes, one Pithecus, journeying to his own country of *Pithecusa*, the Land of Apes, and Don Psittaco believes himself called

> *wisdom sage to show,*
> *And with his sacred lore to wash the spot*
> *Of youthful blemishes,*

—a belief which a wise man will not impetuously entertain. This fresh opportunity to talk is an irresistible temptation, and Pithecus gives 'mimicall attention' to the words of Psittaco that have been got by 'paper stealth'. They are not the counsels of mature experience nor do they convey any coherent meaning to the gaping youngster, until he is arrested by a reference to

> *the shape divine*
> *Which Adam's children have.*

He gathers that Psittaco is extolling man as Lord of Creation and he notes how, whenever this reverend speaker utters the Divine Name, he piously lifts his eyes to heaven. Master Ape, whose ignorance of Religion is profound, concludes that God is 'a thought above the Moon', and 'straight with sanctimonious grace' raises his eyes also. He is the feather-brained youth of all time, with no opinions of his own on the serious concerns of life: hardly, indeed, aware that there are such concerns. Ape-like, he adapts himself to the company of the moment; adopts its conventions and, being devoid of critical faculty, accepts its suggestions, if only his vanity be sufficiently flattered.

HAMLET: *Do you see yonder cloud that's almost in shape of a camel?*

POLONIUS: *By the mass, and 'tis like a camel, indeed.*

HAMLET: *Methinks it is like a weasel.*
POLONIUS: *It is backed like a weasel.*
HAMLET: *Or like a whale?*
POLONIUS: *Very like a whale.*[22]

Pithecus, the perfect Ape! In justice to Polonius, be it said, he was probably playing up to what he took to be madness in Hamlet.

Out of the 'Parrot's' spate of verbiage a glimmer of meaning reaches the youth's addled mind, playing round the words,

> *the Shape divine,*
> *Which Adam had from God,*

and which Adam's progeny has inherited. His imagination is fired. Had he had the genius he might have anticipated Milton:

> *Two of far nobler shape, erect and tall,*
> *Godlike erect, with native honour clad*
> *In naked majesty, seemed lords of all,*
> *And worthy seemed: for in their looks divine*
> *The image of their glorious Maker shone* ...[23]
>
> *Adam the goodliest man of men since born*
> *His sons, the fairest of her daughters Eve.*[24]

Pithecus is not interested in Eve ... as yet! But Milton's picture of Adam is lambent in his mind and he sees himself as the latest specimen of the ancestral stock: the God-like inheritor of this physical beauty; he

> *phansies his sweet face with heavenly hue to shine;*

so

> *He pinched his hat, and from his horse's side*
> *Stretched forth his russet legs, himself inclined*
> *Now here, now there, and most exactly eyed*
> *His comely lineaments, that he might find*
> *What ever beauty else he had not mind [observed]*
> *As yet in his fair corse [body].*

A seventeenth-century Narcissus, in love with his own beauty, whose counterparts More would certainly know in Cambridge! νάρκισσος, the bloom with *narcotic* properties! —so that

spem sine corpore amat, corpus putat esse, quod umbra est;[25]

—an unsubstantial hope he loves and regards as substance what is mere shadow—wherefore great grace from God is needed for his salvation. The distinction between himself and Deity is wearing thin and he looks like becoming the latest recruit to that insidious theosophy that equates man with God; not necessarily God with man, for there are some transcendental equations that look less convincing when their terms are transposed. To a humorist like More such a theosophy is impossible; he would have delighted in Kierkegaard's annihilating comment:

It is a comical thought that the poor philosopher (or theologian) who just after setting down one of his profoundest sentences must turn from his desk to sneeze, should confuse himself with the Infinite Spectator of all time and all existence.[26]

It is at least equally comical when a callow youth, because he is in love with his own body and its beauty, verges upon the same confusion. Ovid knew him, as we have seen, two thousand years ago, and left him in the Underworld, there to contemplate to all eternity the Beatific Vision of Himself: a retributive and poetic form of justice worthy of the imagination of Dante!

tum quoque se, postquam est inferna sede receptus,
in Stygia spectabat aqua:[27]

—and even after he had been received into the Underworld he continued to gaze upon his reflection in the waters of the Styx. True, there were voices of wisdom and experience sounding through the land, but not all heard nor did all who heard take heed. John Donne, being dead, yet eloquently spoke:

Propose this body to thy consideration in the highest exaltation thereof; as it is the Temple of the Holy Ghost: Nay, not in a metaphor, or comparison of a Temple, or any other similitudinary thing, but as it was really and truly the very body of God, in the person of Christ, and yet this body must wither, must decay, must languish, must perish. When Goliath had armed and fortified this body, and Jezebel had painted and perfumed this body, and Dives had pampered and larded this body, as God said to Ezekiel, when he brought him to the dry bones, . . . *Sonne of Man, doest thou thinke these bones can live?* They said in their hearts to all the world, Can these bodies die? And they are dead. Jezebel's dust is not amber, nor Goliath's dust *Terra sigillata*, Medicinall; nor does the Serpent, whose meat they are both, finde any better rellish in *Dives* dust, than in *Lazarus*.[28]

Wise words, over whose truth it is well at times to ponder, that we mistake not the shadow for the substance, nor, beholding the strength and beauty of the human body, adore it as the whole. Milton's *Eve* tells how such temptation came to her almost in the moment of her self-realization as a human being, with the same fascination as to Narcissus. Having reached a 'liquid plain', she says:

> *I thither went*
> *With unexperienced thought, and laid me down*
> *On the green bank, to look into the clear*
> *Smooth lake, that to me seemed another sky.*
> *As I bent down to look, just opposite*
>
> *A shape within the wat'ry gleam appeared,*
> *Bending to look on me: I started back,*
> *It started back; but pleased I soon returned,*
> *Pleased it returned as soon with answering looks*
> *Of sympathy and love: there I had fixed*
> *Mine eyes till now, and pined with vain desire,*
> *Had not a voice thus warned me,'What thou seest,*
> *What there thou seest, fair creature, is thyself;*
> *With thee it came and goes: but follow me,*
> *And I will bring thee where no shadow stays*
> *Thy coming . . .'*[29]

It was the voice of Adam, older, more experienced, beguiling her from the illusory. If any voice within was warning Pithecus he heeded it not; this was for him an hour of hilarity and *gaieté de cœur* and he let all else go by.

Mnemon enjoys all this immensely and we can almost hear him chuckling, 'Lord! What fools these mortals be!'

With the departure of Pithecus, Don Psittaco is silent and disconcerted. Parrot and ape do not jump together; there is no bridge between the aviary and the monkey-house, nor any lingo common to all the inmates of this biological *collegium*. Mnemon seeks to rouse his companion from his torpor by drawing him out in talk. He is preassured of success, knowing that

> *to speak he had great list.*

Don Psittaco is an anticipation, in some respects, of Bunyan's Mr. Talkative, who, in response to Faithful's question, 'What is that one thing that we shall at this time found our discourse upon?', replies:

What you will. I will talk of things heavenly or things earthly; things moral or things evangelical; things sacred or things profane; things past or things to come; things foreign or things at home; things more essential or things circumstantial; provided that all be done to our profit.[30]

How shrewd and observant Bunyan is! Did you notice how Talkative changed the 'we' of Faithful's question to 'I' in his answer? The conversation is going to be a monologue, as conversations occasionally are, to the glory of Talkative. Christian, however, knows this man. 'Religion hath no place in his heart, or house, or conversation; all he hath lieth in his tongue; and his religion is to make a noise therewith' —a description more devastating than Dryden's of men

> *who think too little and who talk too much,*[31]

or George Crabbe's, of a wife in one of his 'Tales', who

> *could not think, but would not cease to speak.*[32]

So both More and Bunyan capture each his specimen of the *genus loquax* and exhibit it for the delectation of posterity.

Don Psittaco at once revives under this apparently genial but in reality satirical encouragement. The Don Psittacos and Talkatives of the world are usually as impervious to satire as the Teutonic mind is to the humour of *Alice in Wonderland* or a *Punch* cartoon. 'I don't see the point of it,' they protest; 'Exactly!' we reply, 'that *is* the point of it'; and they retire more mystified than ever. It is, however, good that we should keep in mind the caution of Dean Swift—and who, in these matters, could speak with greater authority?—'Satire is a sort of glass, wherein beholders do generally discover everybody's face but their own.'[33]

At Mnemon's suggestion Don Psittaco discourses on the surpassing glories of his beloved *Psittacusa*, speaking with great pedantry and prolixity. Loftily he dismisses Mnemon as a 'country swain' when he attempts to interject a remark. Mnemon, hugely delighted and thoroughly at ease in his awareness of his own intellectual superiority, assumes the deadly Socratic pose of complete ignorance and advances innocent-looking but dangerous questions, to which Don Psittaco gives his shallow and still condescending replies. He

> *straight . . . to higher perch, like bird in cage,*
> *Did skip, and sang of etern Destiny;* [eternal Destiny]
> *Of sight and foresight he with countenance sage*
> *Did speak, and did unfold God's secrecy,*
> *And left untouched no hidden mystery.*
>
> *I lowly louting* [bowing] *held my cap in hand;*

whereupon Don Psittaco, perhaps uneasily suspicious, asks what this sudden act of courtesy means and thus provokes some of Mnemon's shafts of keenest irony:

> *I pardon crave, said I, for manners fond;*
> *You are Heaven's Privy-Counsellor, I understand,*

*Which I wist not before: so deep insight
Into the hidden things of God who can
Attain unto, without that quickening spright* [spirit]
Of the true God? ...

*Therefore, as the sacred seat of the Deity,
I unto you seemly behaviour make,
If you be such as you may seem to be.*

Even such extravagant adulation as this the infatuated Don Psittaco greedily sucks in, with never an inkling of its mockery:

> *For he full forward was all to assume
> That might him gild with glory.*

Silence reigns once more and we see these undeclared antagonists more clearly: Don Psittaco, the man wallowing in his ability to prate in parrot speech and so impress the ignorant and gullible among mankind, and Mnemon, to whom all true knowledge is humbling in its effects and inseparable from life, being itself a living growth.

Ritualism, either in association with Religion or as a substitute for it, now becomes the object of More's satirical consideration. The two travellers, still in *Psittacusa*, approach a thickly hedged enclosure and Don Psittaco invites Mnemon to peer between the branches and view the scene within. We presently discover that it is through the windows of a Cathedral Church that the travellers are really looking, and what they see is described allegorically in terms of natural objects: sometimes with touches of beauty more characteristic of the Nature poetry of a later age, and through all there is the ripple of piquant humour.

A service, conducted with Laudian high ceremonial, is in progress, and the King, the titular Head of the Church, is present. The 'trimly decked close', with its 'grassy pavement', is the Church. The eastern end is reached by steps which men climb 'to do their holy things'—'O sight divine!'

comments Mnemon. In the middle of this 'highest flore' is 'a large green turf squared out, all fresh and fair', the altar, 'adorned with every glittering flower'. At each end of it stands a 'Torchwort', a candle,

> *Whose yellow flames small light did cast abroad,*
> *But yet a pleasant show they yield the eye.*

Near by stands a 'hollow oak', the pulpit, with 'soft mosse', the cushion, growing round its edge. Then we see the 'wood-queristers' sitting in a row and sweetly singing,

> *while Boreas* [the organ] *did blow*
> *Above their heads, with various whistling....*

Other birds, the officiating clergy,

> *with gold and purple feathers gaily dight,*

are 'ranked aloft', and amongst these the Eagle, viz., the Monarch,

> *doth assume*
> *The highest sprig, for it is his by right.*

There, in his 'green cabinet', he surveys the assembled congregation. The 'Quire' chants a 'loud song ... tuned to the whistling of the hollow wind', and then out steps

> *a gay Pye* [magpie] *in his rich attire;*
> *The snowy white with the black satin shined;*
> *On his head a silken cap he wore unlined.*
> *When he had hopped to the middle floor*
> *His bowing head right lowly he inclined,*
> *As if some Deity he did adore,*
> *And seemly gestures make, courting the Heavenly power;*

—apparently a description of the service known as sung mattins.

This 'magpie', an uncompromising ritualist, is at once the object of Don Psittaco's scorn and Mnemon's ridicule, to whom his antics are void of significance. Having 'cringed toward the east' the 'Pye' ascends the pulpit, where he

> *thrice congied [bowed] after his ascent,*
> *With posture changed from the East to the Occident,*
> *Thrice bowed he down and easily thrice he rose;*
> *Bowed down so low as if it had been his intent*
> *On the green moss to wipe his swarthy nose.*
> *Anon he chatters loud, but why himself best knows.*

The current view of the pulpit and the sermon was far below that of Cowper in the following century.

> *I say the pulpit . . .*
> *Must stand acknowledged, while the world shall stand,*
> *The most important and effectual guard,*
> *Support and ornament of virtue's cause.*
> *There stands the messenger of truth. There stands*
> *The legate of the skies; his theme divine,*
> *His office sacred, his credentials clear.*
> *By him, the violated law speaks out*
> *Its thunders, and by him, in strains as sweet*
> *As angels use, the Gospel whispers peace.*
> *He 'stablishes the strong, restores the weak,*
> *Reclaims the wanderer, binds the broken heart. . . .*[34]

This is high, healthy doctrine, and no Church that embraces it in its belief and practice can be negligible in the scheme of things. Divines of More's day, like John Donne, Jeremy Taylor, and Richard Baxter held it; they exalted the pulpit and preached 'as a dying man to dying men'; but many of their contemporaries, had they lived a century later, would have come under the lash of that same William Cowper's tongue, as being

> *things that mount the rostrum with a skip,*
> *And then skip down again; pronounce a text,*
> *Cry—hem! and, reading what they never wrote,*
> *Just fifteen minutes, huddle up their work,*
> *And with a well-bred whisper close the scene!*[35]

In such wise the 'Pye' seems to have 'preached'. Mnemon is also astonished at

> *so unexpected Uniformity*
> *And such a semblance of due piety,*

as also at the respective antics of the 'Crows' and 'Daws', that is, the ordinary men and women of this ornithological congregation:

> *for every Crow, as when he cries for rain,*
> *Did eastward nod; and every Daw we see,*
> *When they first entered that grassy Plain,*
> *With shaking wings and bended bills* [*viz., curtseying*] *adored the same.*

Feigning ignorance and bewilderment Mnemon calls upon Don Psittaco to explain the

> *mystery*
> *Which lieth hid in this strange, uncouth show,*

and Psittaco, as we should expect, is eager to oblige. Although they are his fellow countrymen he regards these religionists with bitter animosity. Having stolidly explained to Mnemon that what appear as birds are really human beings—a proceeding which reveals him as a man devoid alike of humour and imagination—he informs Mnemon that the 'Pye' is a certain Don Pico, thus changing his mental and spiritual qualities from those of a magpie to those of a woodpecker. Which of these names is the more complimentary let our ornithologists declare. All Don Psittaco's puritanical hatred of ritualism in religion is concentrated into his description of Don Pico, and Mnemon, in partial agreement only, lures him on by incisive questioning. He disclaims perfect understanding of Don Pico's antics, but presumes that, inasmuch as he bowed but once to the altar and gave 'a triple nod' to the Eagle, the latter is really his God: that is, the monarch, as titular Head of the Church. Mnemon suggests that these three nods may be of courtesy rather than worship, due to 'the seemly graces' of the King, but Psittaco objects that such use of 'holy gestures' would be 'impious flattery'. Mnemon then ironically urges that possibly, through this act of homage to the King, Don Pico is more nearly approaching God, or thinks he is, for there were those in Stuart England who held that all honour paid to the Monarch was really honour paid to the Deity. So for Mnemon it still remains a mystery, why Don Pico should be moved

> *that solemn service with four ducks to fill,*
> *But one before, the other three behind.*

Don Psittaco then attempts another explanation, which is no explanation at all and is quite irrelevant to the matter under immediate discussion. Pico, he asserts, has been blinded by superstition and flattery; he domineers in outrageous fashion over *Psittacusa* and this supremacy Don Psittaco and his associates long to destroy. His enthusiasm kindles at the prospect of a land free from the yoke of ritualism. Then would come the opportunity for anti-ritualists like himself to compel men to accept spiritual truth.

> *O, had we once the power in our hands,*
> *How carefully we the youth would catechise,*
> *. . . and would devise*
> *Set forms of Truth, on Discipline advise,*
> *That unto both all men might needs conform.*

Here Don Psittaco speaks for those who, like the Presbyterian party of the day, favoured a forced conformity both in Faith and Discipline. Mnemon is the eternal rebel against any such coercion or bondage. Though an ordained minister of the Church of England More had, in these matters, the spirit of the Independents:

But what [Mnemon *asks*], *if any tender heart denies?*

that is, what if a man's conscience and intelligence revolt

against your imposed religious faith and ecclesiastical discipline?, and the answer is, in effect, 'So much the worse for his tender heart and his conscience';

> *If he will his own fortunes overturn,*
> *It cannot well be helped,* we must be uniform.

So now the secret is out. This hater of ritual and lover of freedom is, equally with those whom he censures and despises, an intense fanatic, prepared to enforce uniformity at all costs; that is, uniformity in *his* faith and *his* practice, and all this, as he insists, according to the Divine will. Every time this man opens his mouth he delivers himself more irretrievably into the power of one beside whom he is a mental popinjay and who may at any moment turn and rend him. Mnemon, however, has thus far preferred to observe the ancient feline ritual preparatory to a kill. Having pointed out that Don Pico and Don Psittaco agree as to the necessity for uniformity, Mnemon puts two questions to his companion: 1, Is it because he is perfectly certain that he himself has the truth of these matters that he would compel universal assent and compliance? 2, If he does not claim this certainty, will he still visit with pains and penalties those who cannot assent to his propositions? Psittaco's reply is concise and unambiguous:

> *We for certain know;*

and then the cajoling voice of Mnemon continues:

> *how know you those things for certainty?*
> *By Reason, Scripture, or the Spirit divine,*
> *Or lastly by Church's Authority?*

So he brings Don Psittaco up peremptorily before the age-long question, 'On what authority believest thou these things?', and he is nonplussed.

> *With that Don Psittaco cast up his eyes,*
> *Brimful of thoughts to solve this knot of mine.*

Again fortune is kind to this man, for in the very moment of his discomfiture two old friends approach and stay to converse. Both are clerics. Don Graculo—the Reverend Mr. Jackdaw—is dressed in black, rides a black, lean, fiery jade, wears a cap which is 'a dry wall-nut shell to fence his wit', and is a representative of the rationalist approach to religion, a man with a mind

well appointed against every doubt.

There is nothing animating or original about him. He professes to maintain the tradition of the medieval Schoolmen, observing their rules of logic and rhetoric, and, for him, life and religion attend at their assize.

His companion is Don Corvino—Dean Raven!—Bird of unhappy omen!—who rides a fat, 'resty' [restful] jade

that neighed loud,

and the rest of the description is too delicious to be omitted.

His rider was not lean.
His black, plump belly fairly outward swayed,
And pressed somewhat hard upon the horse's mane.
Most like, methought, to a Cathedral Dean.
A man of prudence and great courtesy,
And wisely in the world he knew to glean.
His sweaty neck did shine right greasily;
Top heavy was his head with earthly policy.

We recognize him at once, this obese ecclesiastic, man of the world, prudent and courteous, a good trencher-man, whose interest is less in religion than in the perquisites and arabesques of the priestly office. No further introduction is necessary. He is the digest of all the Archdeacon Grantlys that Crockford ever knew.[36]

A Dean so various that he seemed to be
Not one, but sundry Deans' epitome.[37]

He is concerned above everything to preserve and augment the temporalities of ecclesiastical office and would have agreed heartily with Disraeli that 'the Church of England is not a mere depository of doctrine'; it is also the holder of valuable properties, the administrator of extensive emoluments and benefactions and the legatee of notable rights and privileges. He and Graculo are a strange pair of friends, and although their friendship with Psittaco is wearing thin, this the three have in common:

> *they all dearly hug dominion,*
> *And love to hold men's consciences in awe,*
> *Each standing stiff in his opinion*
> *In holy things, against all contradiction.*

Corvino and Psittaco are chiefly united in this, that they

> *confidently preach*
> *Unless there be a form which men must teach*
> *Of sound opinions (each meaning his own),*
> *But to be left free to doubt and counter speech,*
> *Authority is lost, our trade is gone,*
> *Our Tyrian wares forsaken, we, alas! shall moan,*
>
> *Or at the best our life will bitter be:*
> *For we must toil to make our doctrine good;*
> *Which will impair the flesh and weak the knee;*
> *Our mind cannot attend our trencher food,*
> *Nor be let loose to sue the worldly good.*

They have, at any rate, the virtue of frankness. Here is accusation direct from the mouth of the accused. These two ecclesiastics—we except Graculo from the fullness of this charge—are mentally indolent, if not incapable. Whatever intellectual powers they may once have possessed have become atrophied by gross self-indulgence, beyond all prospect of recovery. Argument they shun like the plague, and if reluctantly drawn into it they collapse, as we shall presently see, before the opening gambit of their opponent. They are the vanguard of a host of ecclesiastics who meet us in the following century and who have their representatives in every age and in almost every religious community: men who would ridicule the modest request of one who should say: 'Put me, I pray thee, into one of the priests' offices, that I may eat a *morsel of bread.*'[38] They are further unpleasantly haunted by the conviction that, if there is to be 'Conscience-freedom, Christian liberty', their day will be done, for men will despise their office and flout their authority, lacking, as these do, the confirmation of a holy life. Horrible thought!

which in good sooth a harder task will be.

The stage is now set for the grand debate, if debate it can be called, on the Seat of Authority in Religion, ever a vital question and specially so in More's day. It is Don Psittaco who rather astutely drops the apple of discord after it had been foisted upon him, to his great discomfort, by Mnemon. 'Brethren,' he says, holding Corvino by his 'holy belt',

> *one thing perplexeth sore*
> *My reason weak and puzzled thoughts. . . .*
> *Tell then, ye learned Clerks, which of these four,*
> *To wit, from Scripture, Church authority,*
> *God's Spirit, or man's Reason is Faith's Certainty.*

'Dean' Corvino responds without hesitation. This is no matter for debate, of which he is obviously incapable; he *pontificates*, as the Corvinos usually do:

> *all belief is solved* [resolved] *at last*
> *Into the Church, nor may the people rude,*
> *Nor learned wit, her honour dare to blast,*
> *Nor scrupulous thoughts nor doubtful queries out to cast.*

So we have the doctrine of an infallible, totalitarian Church bluntly and nakedly stated; a denial to man of all freedom of thought and action in his spiritual life. *Clericus locutus est; causa finita est.*

But Corvino has reckoned without due regard to Graculo, who is theologically rather than ecclesiastically minded; who scorns oracular pronouncements and brooks no dictate other than that of Reason. Much of his 'reasoning' is illicit, but he is blandly unaware of it. We feel that his conclusions are predetermined and if the argument fails to establish them, so much the worse for the argument. We stand aside and enjoy the fun with Mnemon.

Straightway Graculo plunges into the discussion 'with eyes as fierce as ferret', and asserts, with reason, that if each national Church were, in this high-handed fashion, to impose its official formularies and schemes of discipline upon the people, these must continue for ever unchanged and incapable of progress, idolaters remaining idolaters; Indians, Indians; Turks, Turks; to which Corvino, the naïve simpleton, replies:

> *I give not this infallibility*
> *To every Church, but only to our own;*
> *Full witness to herself of all the truths she'll own;*

upon which Graculo insinuates:

> *That then is truth which she will say is true.*
> *But not unless her the true Church thou hold.*
> *How knowest thou then her such, good Corvin show;*

which drives Corvino to the ancient device of declaring that these matters are too sacred for discussion: a sure sign of defeat!

> *Friend* Graculo, *in talk we be too bold.*

However true Pascal's famous words may be in regard to man's personal religion, *Le cœur a ses raisons, que la raison ne connoît pas,* the Graculos quite rightly refuse to accept them in the region of ecclesiastical authority.*

Very conveniently Corvino makes the discovery at this moment that he and his horse are taking cold: perhaps in the feet, though he does not say so. Certainly the situation

* cf. Swift's *Tale of a Tub*, §2: the 'Broomstick' discussion.

is becoming draughty for him. 'Let's go', he urges, and in the same breath flings out his final answer to Graculo's probings:

> *The Church is true as she herself me told;*

the ultimate statement into which every defence of Corvino's position is resolved. It only remains for Graculo to administer the obvious finishing stroke:

> *A goodly answer! . . .*
> *You dispute in a circle, as all logicians know;*

but the Corvinos are dogmatists and not logicians.

This dialogue has warmed the heart of Don Psittaco, who sees in Graculo a possible confederate, overlooking the fact that unity in opposition does not of necessity imply community of positive ideas and beliefs. Thus fortified by the prospect of so redoubtable an ally, and

> *inly smiling,*
> *To see how Graculo Corvin did o'ercrow,*

Psittaco plucks up courage and makes his contribution:

> *'The truth', said he, 'the Scriptures only show.'*

Graculo, who is greatly enjoying himself, instantly reacts:

> *but who can know*
> *The sense of Scripture without reason sound?,*

and Psittaco, the Bibliolater, replies:

> *The Scripture is both key and treasure too;*
> *It opes itself. . . .*
> *This place with that compared. This is the strongest ground.*

'But', retorts Graculo,

> *what with judgement doth them both compare?*
> *Is it reason or unreasonableness, I pray.*

This is too deep for Don Psittaco, who is quite unable to

detect his opponent's illicit use of the word 'reason', and he retires from the contest without a struggle:

> *you so subtil are,*
> *I list not with such cunning wits to play.*

At this point, with Graculo puffing his polemics over his so easily discomfited opponents, Mnemon ventures to speak. His apparent humility and his deference to his auditors would have put less pompous persons on their guard. Describing himself as 'a stranger wight',

> *but homely bred, as yet unripe in years,*
> *Who, conscious of his weaknesses, doth deem*
> *Himself unfit to speak among his peers,*

he plays up to those

> *Whom Age and Arts do equally adorn,*
> *And solemn habit no small semblance bears*
> *Of highest knowledge,*

and craves 'a word or two to speak'. Don Psittaco, flattered, utters a condescending 'Say on'.

Now whilst Don Pico with his elaborate ritual, Don Corvino with his infallible Church and Don Psittaco with his infallible Bible are in the main figures of fun, as they were bound to be for anyone of the Christian-Platonist tradition, Don Graculo is an opponent more seriously to be reckoned with. He is the seventeenth-century rationalist ecclesiastic, fighting the rearguard action of medieval Scholasticism, and men chosen for rearguard actions, if under a wise leader, are not utter fools. They must be stubborn, tough, good fighters, with more than a touch of fanaticism for their cause. Graculo's main weapon is one with which his predecessors were wont to work havoc in the ranks of their opponents, the so-called Law of Contradiction, as enunciated by Aristotle: that the same attribute cannot, at the same time, be both affirmed and denied of the same subject; a statement which is not quite so simple and obvious as it at first appears. We noticed just now how he used it, though illicitly [for reason and unreasonableness in this sense are not complete contradictories nor are reason and reasonableness by any means synonyms], to administer the *coup de grâce* to Don Psittaco, by asking, 'In the interpretation of Scripture do you use Reason or Unreasonableness?' It is the old trick of the false dilemma. 'Choose,' insists Graculo, 'you can't have it both ways.' Don Psittaco, believing that he is confined to one of these alternatives and knowing that whichever he chooses it means the loss of his case, retires from the contest.

Mnemon now proceeds to demolish this dilemma, not by asking Graculo to define his terms, but by insisting that there is a third alternative which is neither Reason nor Unreason, and Graculo at once interrupts to point out that a term which is neither rational nor irrational is an impossibility. Undeterred, Mnemon contends that the Spirit of God is an interpreter of the Scriptures and the final authority in matters of faith, and that, applied to Him, such words as Reason and Unreason are irrelevant, as He moves in a region more spacious than that in which they function. Corvino now intervenes in the conversation for a moment; he 'foamed like his champing jade' and spat out that Mnemon was 'a very silly wight', mad through melancholy and 'unto private spirits [private judgement] all holy truth betrayed'. We are glad that he spoke, for he evoked in Mnemon's reply some of More's most exalted lines:

> *God's Spirit is no private, empty shade,*
> *But that great Ghost that fills both earth and sky,*
> *And through the boundless Universe doth lie,*
> *Shining through purged hearts and simple minds,*
> *When doubling clouds of thick hypocrisy*
> *Be blown away with strongly brushing winds;*
> *Who first this tempest feels, the Sun he after finds.*

This, he declares, is the Doctrine of the Holy Spirit, which has inspired men to holy living and guided them in their search for truth, and where it has been denied or men have been indifferent and merely believed

> *as the Church believes,*
> *Never expecting any other light,*

the result has been loose living, without hope of any inward witness of the Spirit.

At this the three friends drop their differences for the time being and unite to face this contumacious upstart who dares to attack what they hold so dear. Graculo both leads and sustains the assault and insists that the debate be conducted with due deference to Aristotle; they must

> *dispute in figure and in mood,*
> *And stiffly with smart syllogisms fight,*

and to this Mnemon agrees.

The discussion then proceeds as follows. Graculo asserts that the meaning of Scripture can only be ascertained by Reason and challenges Mnemon to produce a single argument to the contrary. More, we must remember, was a typical seventeenth-century intellectual, in that he shared the growing distrust in pure Reason to arrive at all Truth. The new Philosophy and its technique were congenial to him and we may be sure that he heartily agreed with Sir Francis Bacon, one of its leading exponents:

> The philosophy we principally received from the Greeks must be acknowledged puerile, or rather talkative, than generative—as being fruitful in controversies, but barren of effects.
> The understanding, left to itself, ought always to be suspected. . . . Logic . . . by no means reaches the subtilty of nature;[39]

which is to say, that all scientific theories and philosophical judgements must be referred, for the establishing of their validity, to nature, and not remain merely the result of mental processes operating as it were *in vacuo*, which those of both classical and medieval times mainly were, not excepting a philosophico-scientific system as brilliant as that of Lucretius. So Mnemon retorts:

> *Reason . . . in human things may drudge,*
> *But in divine thy soul it may seduce;*

and goes on to support this contention by pointing out that men who reason in syllogistic form often differ in their conclusions, even in matters of high importance. After a long pause Graculo asks what this 'spirit' is, and Mnemon replies that only he who has it knows:

> *'Tis the hid Manna and the graven stone;*

whereupon Corvino exclaims,

> *He canteth . . . come, Grac, let's be gone.*

But 'Grac' is not so minded, and he urges that reasonable matters can only be ascertained through Reason. There the Baconian modernist meets him by pointing out that it is through Sense Perception, not Reason, that men first discover the external world and only then does Reason begin to operate;* as Pope was to have it in the next century:

> *Say first, of God above or man below,*
> *What can we reason but from what we know?*[40]

'Every faculty', says Mnemon,

> *and object have their due Analogy,*
> *Nor can reach further than its proper sphere:*

which he explains as meaning that men do not smell colours, or see sounds, or eat with their ears: entertaining operations, the like of which some of our modern poets alone are competent to perform. He argues that, similarly, Sense and Reason have each a proper sphere and that to attempt to understand 'divine knowledge' by Reason is like listening to

* See p. 79.

the sunshine with one's ear. Graculo wants to know how this spirit can be known and Mnemon points out, with St. Paul, that spiritual things are spiritually discerned, which Graculo criticizes as arguing in a circle. Mnemon then advances an analogous statement, that light is seen by light, perhaps having in mind the words from the thirty-sixth Psalm: 'In Thy light shall we see light.'

Graculo now accepts, for the sake of argument, Mnemon's contention that knowledge is arrived at through Sense (perception) and Right Reason. If the Interpreting Spirit, then, is not Right Reason, it must be Sense, and Mnemon at once replies:

> *Yes, Sense it is. . . .*
> *Sense upon which holy Intelligence*
> *And heavenly Reason and comely Prudence*
>
> *. . . . .*
>
> *Do springen up, through inly [inward] experience*
> *Of God's hid ways, as he doth ope the eyes*
> *Of our dark souls and in our hearts his light enshrine.*

Corvino is still restive to depart while the going is moderately good and Graculo is now like-minded, so he seizes upon Mnemon's reference to Right Reason 'with great joy and jollity', claims the victory on the strength of it and says goodbye;

> *Wherefore he forward goes,*
> *Now more confirmed his Nutshell cap contained*
> *Whatever any living mortal knows.*
> *No longer would he stay, this sweet conceit to lose.*

He is concerned to preserve the precarious peace of his Scholastic cloister, for without are dogs and sorcerers like Hobbes, Descartes, Bacon, and this pestiferous fellow Mnemon. He is the man of Francis Quarles's couplet, impregnable in his conceit:

> *His eye most blind where most it ought to see;*
> *And when his heart's most bound, then thinks himself most free.*[41]

So he grasps the banner of his egoism and waves it aloft in victorious retreat.

Once more Don Psittaco and Mnemon are alone together. This discussion has shaken the self-confidence of the former and he now declares his belief that only such as are enlightened by the Spirit of God are required to impose religious beliefs and ordinances upon others. He calmly assumes that he and Mnemon, whom he now regards with respectful awe, are thus qualified and called, a suggestion which the latter vigorously repudiates on his own behalf. Mnemon expresses himself as wholly at a loss to understand how compulsion can be exercised in matters of faith at all, for

> *if light divine we know by divine light,*
> *Nor can by any other means it see,*
> *This ties their hands from force that have the spirit.*

Don Psittaco makes the feeble suggestion that without force Church polity would be vain, and Mnemon replies that 'enforced faith' is against Reason, Religion, Sense, and Law.

More now introduces the last issue to be faced in the part of his book which we are considering and he does it in the form of a dialogue between these two travellers. It concerns the distinction between 'Divine Sagacity', in the settling of Christian Doctrine and the Interpretation of Scripture, on the one hand, and 'Enthusiasm' on the other: the claim, that is, to private insight, due to a special indwelling of the Spirit of God, manifesting itself frequently in ecstasies and extravagant proceedings which brought discredit upon religion in the eyes of intelligent people. That is to say, the issue is between a true and a false *method of interpretation,* not, be it noted, between a true and a false exegesis of either Scripture or Doctrine. Don Psittaco occasions this discussion by a sudden reference to a daughter Glaucis (the owl) of whom we have not hitherto heard. Her father is sure that if she had been privileged to hear Mnemon expound his doctrine of the Spirit her 'joyous spright' would have 'danced along'.

Glaucis represents the extreme puritanical 'enthusiasts', each sect claiming to be the receptacle of the Holy Spirit of God and the mouthpiece of Deity. In erotic language Don Psittaco asserts how she would have

> *admired*
> *Thy sifting wit, thy speech and person loved,*
> *Clove to that mouth with melting zeal all fired,*
> *And hung upon those lips so highly inspired,*

to which Mnemon replies that she must be

> *a bold immodest wight*
> *To come so near when not at all desired;*

whereupon her father hastens to explain that Mnemon has mistaken his meaning:

> *I meant no fond salutes, but what is just and right.*

Nevertheless he goes on to suggest the suitability of a match between these two, for

> *by Nature's course*
> *Like join with like: wherefore, right well I ween,*
> *Might I but make the match, it would well beseem.*
> *For your conspiring minds exactly agree*
> *In points, which the wide world through wrath and teen* [grief, injury]
> *Rudely divide, I mean free Liberty.*

All this is as acceptable and flattering to Mnemon as would be a suggestion to the Vicar of Noodleton Parva that he should fraternize with the Plymouth Brethren, because he and they are alike in declining to meet with other Christians at what is supposed to be the Table of the Lord. Mnemon declines, because 'our grounds' for this apparent agreement 'farre different be'. He knows this Glaucis only too well, a pseudo-Christianized version of the ancient Bacchæ, those

Deity-inflamed women, 'wild things', as Euripides has it, who

> *knelt*
> *And ramped and gloried, and the wilderness*
> *Was filled with moving voices and dim stress.*[42]

With deft, vivid strokes Mnemon depicts these crack-brained fanatics in a description of Don Psittaco's daughter, who

> *So dexterously can pray and prophesy,*
> *And lectures read of dread mortality,*
> *Clasping her palms with fatal noise and shrieks.*

She lives, he maintains, in a fool's Paradise, bereft of sense and reason, being, with her self-deceived followers, like the

> *mistaken Cat that licked the file,*
> *And drawing blood, incessantly did toil*
> *To suck that sweet.*

They regard their 'enthusiasm' as an outpouring of the Spirit of God,

> *and count themselves His only choice Offspring,*
> *Upon no count but that their count is so.*

These sectaries, holding in their own peculiar fashion the doctrines of the Eternal Decrees, are exhibiting their logical consequences for all to see. Inasmuch as Glaucis is either immutably saved or immutably damned, her liberty is unfettered by any moral or other restraints. Her father understands the gravity of this indictment and at once professes agreement with Mnemon, turning upon his daughter whose praises and charms he has just been singing. He goes beyond Mnemon in his condemnation and bitterly contradicts almost everything he has previously said. He accuses her of Rapine, Riot, Lust, Covetousness, Pride, Sacrilege, and 'a thousand more disorders'. She and her followers, he complains, claim Divine inspiration in the interpretation of even the most obscure Scripture passages and points of doctrine; even the churches they contemptuously desecrate on the rare occasions when they visit them,

> *with hooting wild*
> *Thou [addressing Glaucis as if she were present] causest uproars,*
>   *and our holy things,*
> *Font, Table, Pulpit, they be all defiled*
> *With thy broad mutings and large squirtings vile.*

'Steady! Steady, old man!', is Mnemon's attitude, who now prepares to defend Glaucis against the excessive vilifications of her unnatural parent:

> *hide such infirmities*
> *From stranger wight: Who would his own dear child*
> *Thus shamefully disgrace? With mine own eyes*
> *Have I thy Glaucis seen, and better things surmise.*

In stinging words he then points out that Glaucis is not defaced out of all likeness to her sire; her excesses are but the natural development of the Calvinistic Puritanism in which she has been instructed and trained by him, so that in reproaching her he is also reproaching himself.

Finally, More, as Mnemon, talks a little about himself and some of his ideas and ways of looking at things. As a boy he had hated hypocrisy and, loving liberty more than life, he had

> *much suspected all that would engage*
> *My heart to their own sect, and free-born soul encage;*

so he fled from the sectaries like a hunted animal. He lets us know that for him there is but one guiding light, that of the true conscience. He sees himself as a citizen of the Cosmos, taught by God and Nature. This 'Nature' is not the carnal appetite of the Pauline Epistles but the 'natural' response on man's part to what is good and the recoil from what is evil. To youth he is very tender, and with Don Psittaco as audience and his Cambridge students in mind, he addresses them in a kind of reverie:

> *Dear lads! How do I love your harmless years,*
> *And melt in heart, while I the Morning-shine*
> *Do view of rising virtue, which appears*
> *In your sweet faces and mild, modest eyes.*
> *Adore that God that doth himself enshrine*
> *In your untainted breasts; and give no ear*
> *To wicked voice that may your souls incline*
> *Unto false peace, or unto fruitless fear,*
> *Lest loosened from your selves, Harpies away you bear.*
>
> *Abstain from censure, seek and you shall find,*
> *Drink your own waters drawn from living well,*
> *Mind in your selves what ill elsewhere you mind,*
> *Deal so with men as you would have them deal,*
> *Honour the Aged that it may go well*
> *With you in Age.* . . .

The two travellers have now come to divergent roads where they part company and we also with them. Mnemon is anxious to leave this uncongenial land of *Psittacusa*, where there is

> *no order but what riches, strength and wit*
> *Prescribe. So bad the good easily confound;*

where life is lived on a basis of self-love and self-interest. 'I am weary', he says, 'of this uncouth place.' So we wave good-bye to him as he journeys to the pleasanter land of *Dizoia* (double livedness) where those who will may follow and meet with him again.

It is not easy to quote from this poem and there are few lines that leap out upon us and draw the response, 'That is beautifully said; it cannot be bettered'. Dean Inge describes More's poetry as 'rough and unmusical',[43] a judgement which requires a little qualification. Plato banished poets from his Ideal Republic, but it is conceivable that he would have found a place for Henry More, for he was a philosopher before he was a poet. Always, for him, his subject is paramount; verse is merely the particular medium of expression which he has chosen. It is unprofitable, nor does it alter facts, to ask if it is the best medium for his purpose, or whether the Spenserian stanza in which he wrote is the most appropriate of verse forms. Some may think not. Verse, especially rhymed verse, limits freedom of expression, though it may impart grace to it, and in treating philosophical subjects a man needs all the spaciousness he can command. He wants the best word, the most explicit phrase, whether it rhymes with some other word or goes euphoniously with some other phrase or not. So also with the rhythm. If the philosophy shirks the rhyme or the rhythm, as it so frequently will, then, for the man who is bent upon utter clarity, these must suffer or go. With More they suffer, which helps to explain Dean Inge's comment. Philosophy refuses to submit to arbitrary canons and conventions of literature and remain true to itself. To man's emotional nature Rhyme and Rhythm may be wings; to Philosophy they may be fetters.

It is of interest to notice that More's place in the world of letters was one of the points at issue between Coleridge and his friend Southey. On this poem Southey writes: 'There is perhaps no other poem in existence, which has so little that is good in it, if it has anything good.' Coleridge comments: '27th December 1819. Mr. J. H. Frere, of all men eminently φιλόκαλος, of the most exquisite taste, observed this very day to me how very grossly Southey had wronged this poem. I cannot understand in what mood Southey could have been: it is so unlike him.'[44]

Elsewhere Southey writes: 'He [More] soon begins to imitate John Bunyan in his nomenclature: but oh! what an imitation of that old king of the tinkers!': on which

Coleridge justly observes: 'False, cruelly false! Again and again I puzzle myself to guess in what most un-Southeyan mood Southey could have been, when he thought and wrote the above!—And the phrase, old king of the Tinkers! applied to the author of the inimitable *Pilgrim's Progress*, that model of beautiful, pure, and harmonious English, no less than of still higher merits, outrages my moral taste.'[45] What a pity it is that Coleridge did not *check up on dates*! Had he done so he could have delivered the *coup de grâce* to Southey, for The Pilgrim's Progress was published in 1678 and More's poem in 1642, that is, thirty-six years earlier than the work which he is charged with imitating.

More's allegory is, of course, reminiscent of Bunyan's, though, in comparison with Bunyan's virile characters his are puppets, lay figures to serve as objects for his ridicule. Apart from Mnemon there is not a sanely religious person among them, and the one woman, though she never actually appears upon the scene, is the least sane of them all. But More's purpose is clear; he is trying by negative methods to present a positive view of true religion. These figures enable him to expose the absurdities and irrelevancies of many of the leading professors of religion of his own day, whose types recur from age to age. Clearly he shows much that the Christian Religion is not and, for the most part, he leaves it to his readers to infer what it is. Occasionally, as in the lines on those who partake of the life of God:

> *Souls that of His own good life partake*
> *He loves as His own self.* . . .[46]

and on the Spirit of God:

> *That great Ghost that fills both earth and sky.* . . .[47]

he speaks positively, magniloquently and with a depth of feeling that rouses our responsive emotion. We get the impression that, in the main, he is holding himself in check. He gives the stage to his puppets that, by their foolish vapourings, his readers may be led to turn with disgust from religious artificialities and unrealities to that living, inward experience of the love and power of God which More himself enjoyed. In the main, his most appreciative readers would be those who stood in no need of such a conversion; who already looked at the religious world of their day in much the same way as More, and would find pleasure in having their own ideas expressed in so lively a fashion. The Picos, Psittacos, Corvinos, and Graculos would go on their way, never recognizing themselves in the mirror which More held before them; satire alone can never convict these men of ignorance and the life of false values that springs therefrom. In Psittaco alone is there any change, but his changes are as stupid as the man himself, all based on a complete misunderstanding of Mnemon's words and in no sense the kind of reaction that More, in his person, must have desired to see.

Some people may question the use of satire in the advocacy of religious truth but it has its place; it startles some minds into alert attention and, as it were, 'tattoos' its matter into the memory, thus, in some degree, influencing the life. A. N. Whitehead, in his *Adventures of Ideas*, says:

The last flicker of originality is exhibited by the survival of satire. Satire does not necessarily imply a decadent society, though it flourishes upon the outworn features in the social system. [He instances various epochs.] . . . Satire is the last flicker of originality in a passing epoch as it faces the onroad of staleness and boredom.[48]

The statement is not inapplicable to More. He lived in an age when spiritual fervour was yielding to the hard dogmatism of bitterly opposed factions and men were contending for ritualistic and ecclesiastical forms from which the spirit of true religion had almost departed. Society was facing toward the age of Deism with its staleness and boredom where a living and inspiring faith should have been operative.

More was no *de facto* anti-sectarian; he was *anti* whatever is false, absurd, and irrelevant in any sect whatever. He was deeply concerned about ceremonial and authority in Religion, and the evil effects which these, in any extreme or irrational form, are bound to have upon the practice of vital religion. He expresses himself very clearly on these matters:

All that I mean is this: That neither eager Promoting of Opinion or Ceremony, nor the earnest opposing of the same, no, not the acuteness of Reason, nor yet a strong if naked conceit, that we have the Spirit of God, can excuse a man from being in any better condition than in the Land of Brutes, or in the mere animal nature.[49]

Here, in language appropriate to his cast of mind, More is expressing what were to be the convictions of the religious leaders of the succeeding century, and there is no presumption in claiming him as one of the minor heralds of the Methodist Revival of Religion. As we have noted, John Wesley knew and appreciated the writings of the Cambridge school and in Vol. XXIII of his *Christian Library* he printed one of Henry More's written, but probably never preached, sermons. He also adapted some of his hymns for the use of his own followers and in so doing improved them. The Methodist Hymn-book of 1933 contains two of these, as they appeared in *A Collection of Hymns for the Use of the People called Methodists*, issued in 1779. They are,

> *Father, if justly still we claim*
>   *To us and ours the promise made,*
> *To us be graciously the same,*
>   *And crown with living fire our head;*[50]

and

> *On all the earth Thy Spirit shower;*
>   *The earth in righteousness renew;*
> *Thy kingdom come, and hell's o'erpower,*
>   *And to Thy sceptre all subdue.*[51]

The latest book also contains one hymn much as More wrote it:

> *God is ascended up on high,*
> *With merry noise of trumpet's sound,*
> *And princely seated in the sky,*
> *Rules over all the world around.*[52]

In his *Address to the Clergy* (6th February 1756), John Wesley suggests a number of questions that clergymen should put to themselves in order to test their intellectual fitness for their calling. One of them is:

Am I a tolerable master of the sciences? Have I gone through the very gate of them, Logic?

He then passes on to Metaphysics:

Have I conquered so much of it (Metaphysics), as to clear my apprehension and range my ideas under proper heads; so much as enables me to read *with ease and pleasure, as well as profit*, Dr. Henry More's Works?[53]

More's close familiarity with the Bible is everywhere apparent in his writings; the 'language of Zion' flows naturally from his heart through his pen. Of dogmatic theology there is little trace in his work. His 'God' was too 'big' to be confined within the various dogmatic formulæ which that age bandied from lip to lip and about which men argued with a bitterness that astonishes us today. Henry More stands outside the arena of conflict. In the new and richer context of the Christian Faith and Experience, he had discovered a truth that Æschylus, more than two thousand years earlier, had known and attempted to express:

> *He that is righteous, uncompelled and free,*
>   *His life's way taketh*
> *Not without happiness: and utterly*
> *Cast to destruction shall he never be.*

O'er all man's striving variously
God looketh, but, where'er it be,
Gives to the Mean his victory.
And therefore know I and confess,
The doomed child of Godlessness
Is Pride of Man, and Pride's excess;
Only from health of heart shall spring
What men desire, what poets sing,
    Stormless days.[54]

VI

Songs of Spiritual 'Felicitie'

Thomas Traherne—circa 1636–74

THOMAS TRAHERNE is a standing refutation of Swinburne's contention that 'dead men rise up never':[1] that is, in the sense in which Pope tells us that Shakespeare 'grew immortal in his own despite'.[2] For more than two hundred years it could have been said of Traherne's manuscript poems that

> *untouched the pages lie,*
> *And slumber out their immortality;*[3]

but they *were* immortal and their sleep came to an end. The story of their awakening is a literary romance. The Fairy Prince who broke their slumbers was Mr. Wm. T. Brooke, who, in 1897, purchased two manuscripts of poems from a street bookstall for a few pence. They were at first attributed to Henry Vaughan, but presently their true author was traced. Eventually they passed into the possession of Mr. Bertram Dobell, who tells the full story in his edition of the *Poems* issued in 1903: a story repeated in the charming and enlarged edition of 1932.

Thomas Traherne's personal history is all too briefly told. His father was a shoemaker of Hereford, and shoes are of high and glamorous significance in the realm of childhood's romance, where dwell such ethereal and immortal creatures as Cinderella and the Old Lady who ruled her large and distracting family with parsimony and austerity. It seems that in that shop in Hereford there were not only shoes but dreams to sell, for it came to pass that the shoemaker's son showed himself to be of the spiritual lineage of *Wynken, Blynken,* and *Nod,* who

>   *one night*
> *Sailed off in a wooden shoe—*
> *Sailed on a river of crystal light,*
> *Into a sea of dew;*[4]

a shoe, we feel certain, in whose fashioning his father had taken a proud and loving part and which he had blessed with his prayers. The shoe carried him to Oxford and Brasenose College, probably in 1652, when he was about sixteen years of age. There he graduated in Arts and Divinity and in 1657 was appointed to the living of Credenhill, near Hereford. Ten years later he became chaplain to Sir Orlando Bridgman, the Lord Keeper of the Seals, in whose house in Teddington he died in 1674, and was buried in the parish church. His earthly life was short, about thirty-eight years, but if his writings are any revelation of the man, as they obviously are, it was a very happy one. In the *Meditations* he gives us this glimpse into the secret of his joy:

> When I came into the country (Credenhill), and being seated among silent trees, and meads and hills, had all my time in mine own hands, I resolved to spend it all, whatever it cost me, in search of happiness, and to satiate that burning thirst which Nature had enkindled in me from my youth. In which I was so resolute, that I chose rather to live upon ten pounds a year, and to go in leather clothes, and feed upon bread and water, so that I might have all my time clearly to myself, than to keep many thousands per annum in an estate of life where my time would be devoured in care and labour.[5]

He was a young man of tranquil ambitions, lucent with

> *the light that never was, on sea or land,*
> *The consecration and the poet's dream,*[6]

and the fruit of them was the two volumes that give him an assured place in English literature, the *Poems* and the

Centuries of Meditations. With good reason, discerning critics have found a vein of richer poetry in the latter than in the former, although in form it is prose. In subject matter and sentiment they are very closely related and much of the prose is a thinly disguised paraphrase of the poetry. We shall be concerned with the formal poems alone, as found in the Dobell Folio Manuscript, this apparently containing the poet's work untouched by another hand. They occupy eighty pages of the edition of 1932.

With fascinating intimacy, the verse reveals the writer: his thoughts and speculations; his outlook upon life; his desires and emotions; his pleasures and antipathies; all, in fact, that goes to make up the inner and spiritual life of man. As we read we feel how fluid much of his thought is. Had he lived a few more years all that is best in his work might have crystallized into forms of maturer beauty and been urged with more persuasive power. He is entirely unworldly, largely because he is so amazed at the wonder of his own being in so wonderful a world. This species of self-regard is a healthy one, with no flavour of vainglory. He would have agreed with Robert Louis Stevenson:

> *The world is so full of a number of things,*
> *I'm sure we should all be as happy as kings.*

He himself assuredly was; and the first of these wonders was —HIMSELF. It could hardly be otherwise, for without the grand miracle that 'I am I' nothing else could have meaning or existence, according to a philosophy of Being with which Traherne carried on a brief flirtation, as we shall presently notice.

A rough sequence of thought development in time is discernible in the Poems. He begins with himself before birth, and although he writes glowingly and as a favoured child of Deity, he is thinking of himself in a representative capacity. His wonder at the creation of man and his environment grows and, in effect, he says to us: 'This I *know*, and you may know it too.' It is, though in a different connexion, Charles Wesley's sentiment:

> *What we have felt and seen*
> *With confidence we tell.*

There is no suggestion of personal superiority, but only a deep desire to open the eyes of others to their so often despised or neglected privileges.

The opening poem is a salute to this representative self. Traherne's imagination carries him back to a period prior to his birth:

> *when silent I,*
> *So many thousand thousand years,*
> *Beneath the dust did in a chaos lie,*[7]

but there is a curious lack of consistency in this very time-bound and materialistic conception, for in the next stanza he writes:

> *I that so long*
> *Was nothing from Eternity. . . .*[8]

Ideas of this kind were astir in the minds of some of Traherne's contemporaries, such as Sir Thomas Browne, who expresses himself with a clarity and precision that would be very welcome in Traherne's verse:

That which is the cause of my Election, I hold to be the cause of my Salvation, which was the mercy and beneplacit of God, before I was, or the foundation of the World. *Before Abraham was, I am*, is the saying of Christ; yet is it true in some sense, if I say it of my self; for I was not onely before my self, but Adam, that is, in the Idea of God, and the decree of that Synod held from all Eternity. And in this sense, I say, the World was before the Creation, and at an end before it had a beginning; and thus was I dead before I was alive: though my grave be England, my dying place was Paradise: and Eve miscarried of me before she conceiv'd of Cain.[9]

What mainly interests Traherne is that during this long period of nescience, though, apparently, not non-being,

> *A* GOD *preparing did this glorious store,*
> *The World for me adorn.*[10]

This pre-natal life he regards as a preparation for 'Felicitie', a word which holds for him all the perfume of existence. Then comes the miracle of putting on a mortal body, when

> *From dust I rise,*
> *And out of nothing now awake* . . . ,[11]

a conception of human beginnings which has an interesting affinity with Berdyaev's doctrine of the Meonic.* Perhaps Traherne was too impatient to develop it, for he was more interested in life itself than in speculations about its origins. He was the kind of man that even Charles Darwin was in one transcendent moment, which he describes in a letter to his wife (April 1858):

At last I fell asleep in the grass, and awoke with a chorus of birds singing around me, and squirrels running up the trees, and some woodpeckers laughing, and it was as pleasant and rural a scene as ever I saw, *and I did not care one penny how any of the beasts or birds had been formed.*[12] [Italics are mine.]

Certainly Traherne was a creature of moods, who toyed with the ideas that his fertile mind evolved, but rarely came to final terms with them. It may be that he lost his metaphysical way in the tropical luxuriance of his language and the dazzling radiance of his joy.

He thinks himself back to his earliest days and tries to apprehend the world through the sense organs of a child's body, endowed with the developed intelligence of the mature man; the man's intelligence speaks, as it were, in a baby's frame. He addresses his body:

* See p. 88.

> *These little Limbs,*
> *These Eyes and Hands which here I find,*
> *These rosy Cheeks wherewith my Life begins,*
> *Where have ye been? Behind*
> *What curtain were ye from me hid so long!*
> *Where was? in what abyss, my speaking Tongue?*

A curious fancy! Body and Soul have been leading a separate existence, nor could the lonely soul conceive what joys were awaiting it when its union with the body should take place. I

> *Did little think such joys as Ear or Tongue,*
> *To celebrate or see:*
> *Such Sounds to hear, such Hands to feel, such Feet,*
> *Beneath the skies, on such a ground to meet.*[13]

We need hardly regard this supposition of the pre-existence of a separate Soul and Body as a serious element in his thought, but rather as a poet's passing fancy, through which he expresses his thrilling joy at being alive, with a miraculous body in a miraculous world. His delight at being born is independent of time, place, or circumstance: utterly without the complacency that Gibbon, for example, displays when writing on this theme:

My lot might have been that of a slave, a savage or a peasant: nor can I reflect without pleasure on the bounty of Nature, which cast my birth in a free and civilized country, in an age of science and philosophy, in a family of honourable rank, and decently endowed with the gifts of fortune.[14]

Traherne's joy was less over-weening, more elemental, and sprang from possessions and experiences that were equally accessible to other civilized beings: not from those natural only to a favoured time, place, or social station; it had more of the flavour of Wordsworth's

> *Joy in widest commonalty spread,*[15]

and something also of the abandon and elation of the Greek girls in Sturge Moore's *Chorus:*

> *Pretend to fly*
> *Up into the sky,*
> *Jumping with both feet together,*
> *Holding out like wings*
> *Your sleeves and things,*
> *Feeling as light as a feather,*
> *Never wonder whether*
> *The day be long*
> *Or the night short,*
> *Since all our thought*
> *(Big as the song*
> *Of a brown, fussy bee)*
> *But just fills the flower which we*
> *Each call 'Me'.* [16]

There are, for Traherne, four outstanding wonders: Himself, His Body, the Outer World, and the God who made them all. It is a short but comprehensive list, embracing spiritual and material; animate and inanimate; Divine and human. It is with the exquisite union of his Spirit and his Body that his joy begins, and a part of that joy he experiences in the mere naming of his bodily parts. In addition to his limbs, eyes, hands, cheeks, and feet already mentioned, he dwells on the 'organized joynts', sinews, nostrils, skin, and in his poem *The Person* he reverently reviews them all and contrasts some of them with the clothing and grosser adornments of the body:

> *The Muscles, Fibres, Arteries, and Bones*
> *Are better far than Crowns and Precious Stones.*

'Old Satan' would ensnare him with these things, but in vain. *Video meliora, proboque.*[17] In respect of his bodily parts,

> *Their harmony is far more sweet;*
> *Their beauty true. And these in all my ways*
> *Shall themes become, and organs of Thy praise.*[18]

With St. Paul he believes that the Body was intended to be the Temple of the Holy Spirit of God, and such he is determined his own body shall ever be.

A physically constituted human being, he now begins, through his body, to sense his environment. The wonder of the interplay between the objective world and his own spirit, through the medium of his bodily sense organs, is a theme of which he never tires. That outer world is of Divine workmanship and so is he; at that point he and it are in closest affinity:

> *How like an Angel came I down!*
> *How bright are all things here!*
> *When first among His works I did appear*
> *O how their Glory me did crown!*
> *The World resembled His Eternity,*
> *In which my soul did walk;*
> *And every thing that I did see,*
> *Did with me talk.*[19]

The world of the newly-born is one which God has specially prepared:

> *Into this Eden so divine and fair,*
> *So wide and bright, I come His Son and Heir.*[20]

Nor does it contain anything unworthy of God, for

> *Nothing's truly seen that's mean:*
> *Be it a sand, an acorn, or a bean.*[21]

Traherne never becomes insensible to the wonder of these things being *his*:

> *that they mine should be, who nothing was,*
> *That strangest is of all, yet brought to pass.*[22]

His wonder is comparable with that of Sir Bors, the humble-minded knight of the Round Table, to whom was vouchsafed an utterly unexpected vision of the Holy Grail:

> *and then to me, to me,*
> *... beyond all hopes of mine,*
> *Who scarce had prayed or asked it for myself,*
> *... the sweet Grail*
> *Glided and passed.*[23]

Jesus gives us the sure clue to such experiences: *Blessed are the pure in heart, for they shall see God.* Thus has it ever been. There were many devout souls in Traherne's day to whom the world was a mirror in which they saw the Face of God. John Donne spoke for them in a sermon which he preached at St. Paul's on Easter Day, 1628:

Whatsoever hath any being, is by that very being, a glass in which we see God, who is the root and fountain of all being. The whole frame of nature is the Theatre, the Volume of creatures is the glass, and the light of nature, reason, is our light.[24]

In *The Second Anniversary*, Donne describes Elizabeth Drury —with what accuracy is immaterial—as one

> *Who with God's presence was acquainted so,*
> *(Hearing, and speaking to Him) as to know*
> *His face in any natural stone, or tree,*
> *Better than when in images they be.*[25]

John Hall (1627–56) was also a poet for whom everything in Nature was a showing of God, including even 'lazy Snailes' and 'speechlesse Fishes', and the World itself a Book of Revelation, rather than a mirror:

> *Great Lord, from whom each Tree receaves,*
> *Then paies againe, as rent, his leaves;*
> > *Thou dost in purple set*
> > *The Rose and Violet,*
> *And giv'st the sickly Lilly white,*
> *Yet in them all, Thy name dost write.*[26]

There were men living who remembered Edmund Spenser and who read with a thrill of pleasure, as men always will, his expression of the same faith: a faith that was also theirs:

> *How can we see with feeble eyne*
> *The glory of that Majestie-Divine,*
> *In sight of whom both Sun and Moone are darke,*
> *Comparèd to his least resplendent sparke?*
>
> *The meanes, therefore, which unto us is lent*
> *Him to behold, is on his workes to looke,*
> *Which he hath made in beauty excellent,*
> *And in the same, as in a brasen booke,*
> *To read enregistred in every nooke*
> *His goodnesse, which his beautie doth declare;*
> *For all that's good is beautiful and faire.*[27]

Faith carried such men to dizzy heights of speculation and few, as we shall observe, were more daring in their ventures than Traherne.

In language of ecstasy he dwells lingeringly on Nature's beauties: 'the skies in their magnificence', 'the lively, lovely air':

> *Clouds here and there like wingèd chariots flying,*
> *Flowers ever flourishing, yet always dying....*[28]

> *The World my House, the Creatures were my Goods,*
> *Fields, Mountains, Valleys, Woods,*
> *Men and their Arts to make me rich combine.*[29]

This world, however, is not his private estate, and he invites all and sundry to share it with him, as their birthright and privilege:

> *First then behold the World as thine, and well*
> *Note that where thou dost dwell.*

> *See all the beauty of the spacious Case,*
> *Lift up thy pleased and ravished eyes,*
> *Admire the Glory of the Heavenly place,*
> *And all its blessings prize.*[30]

Nature exists for the service of Man, but in no squalid or vulgarly hedonistic sense.

> *We plough the very Skies, as well*
> *As Earth, the spacious Seas*
> *Are ours; the Stars all gems excel.*
> *The Air was made to please*
> *The souls of Men; devouring fire*
> *Doth feed and quicken Man's desire.*
> *The Orb of Light in its wide circuit moves,*
> *Corn for our food springs out of very mire,*
> *Our fences and fuel grow in woods and groves,*
> *Choice Herbs and Flowers aspire*
> *To kiss our feet; Beasts court our loves.*
> *How glorious is Man's fate!*
> *The Laws of God, the Works He did create,*
> *His ancient Ways, are His, and my Estate.*[31]

To put it bluntly, Traherne believes that the Universe has been made for Man: a belief which may have health-giving and soul-satisfying effect if it is not made a pedestal for a sculptured human being swaggering toward divinity and bawling *Sublimi feriam sidera vertice.*[32]

Thus he delivers himself over to those controversialists whose knees become weak as water at the mere suggestion of a teleological explanation of the Universe, and especially of one which looks to Man as its *telos*. Listen to them, angrily muttering in the background: 'The conceit of this man! What, pray, does he think that *he* is? Does he not know that he is a quite negligible and rather pitiable by-product of the vast machine of the Universe?' Assuredly Thomas Traherne did not know it, nor could ever have been induced to know it. He might, perhaps, have inquired what, if Man is merely a by-product, is the main product of this machine; that for which it was originally constituted: pointing out, also, that a machine is essentially *teleological*. As we retrace his thoughts we know that Traherne lived in a realm that reached 'beyond the sunset, and the baths of all the western stars'; that his horizon could never have been compassed in a mathematical formula, be it ever so exquisite; that had he lived in our more spacious days neither Astrophysics nor Biochemistry would have disillusioned or 'converted' him, nor would awareness of the Space-Time Continuum have marred his 'Felicitie'. He might even have joined the company of the wise and humble-minded of the earth, and found a place for these conceptions among the things that gave him Joy.

There are passages in some of the poems which give the reader the impression that under the stimulus of his joy Traherne is theorizing about the experiences which cause it, though never very seriously or at length. He seeks a kind of extension of his joy beyond the experiences themselves to what he thinks about them. There are surprising hints of a hesitant anticipation of Bishop Berkeley (1685-1753) and his Subjective Idealism, which the famous prelate expounded in such a typical passage as this:

Some truths there are so near and obvious to the mind, that a man need only open his eyes to see them. Such I take this important one to be, to wit, that all the choir of heaven and furniture of the earth, in a word, all those bodies which compose the mighty frame of the world, have not any subsistence without a mind: that their *being* [*esse*] is to be perceived or known: that consequently so long as they are not actually perceived by me, or do not exist in my mind or that of any other *created spirit*, they must either have no existence at all, or else subsist in the mind of some eternal spirit.[33]

The *esse* of things is *percipi*. In that famous formula Berkeley crystallized a philosophy which has perennial attraction for the human spirit.* It cannot be refuted by kicking stones about with Dr. Samuel Johnson[34] nor yet by composing such smart limericks as

> *There once was a man who said, 'God*
> *Must think it exceedingly odd,*
> > *If He finds that this tree*
> > *Continues to be,*
> *When there's no one about in the Quad';*

which evoked the quite apposite Berkeleyan reply:

> *Dear Sir, Your astonishment's odd;*
> *I am always about in the Quad,*
> > *And that's why the tree*
> > *Will continue to be,*
> *Since observed by, yours faithfully, God.*[35]

For the speculative and poetical mind Berkeley's ideas have great attraction; they keep coming into the world picture. A poet as modern as Mr. Walter de la Mare exemplifies this. In *A Riddle*, after a charming description of what he saw and heard one Spring noonday in a 'sea-lulled lane', he reflects:

> *O restless thought,*
> *Contented not! With 'Why' distraught.*
> *Whom asked you then your riddle small?—*
> *'If hither came no man at all*
>
> *'Through this grey-green, sea-haunted lane,*
> *Would it mere blackened naught remain?*
> *Strives it this beauty and life to express*
> *Only in human consciousness?*
>
> *'Or, rather idly breaks he in*
> *To an Eden innocent of sin;*
> *And, prouder than to be afraid,*
> *Forgets his Maker in the made?'*

* See Appendix, p. 194.

Well! Which?—though, be it noted, we are not here presented with two only possible alternatives. So far as the first is concerned the 'hard-headed', practical man, who traffics in his intuitions and stands surety for his own omniscience, *knows*—with Dr. Johnson. But another type of mind stands poised on the same spot, hesitant, pensive, almost reverent, as hovering on the fringe of ultimate mystery that no humanly devised formula can wholly fathom. Was it a pre-natal Berkeley, then nearing the end of his 'thousand thousand years' of silence, who quickened within the soul of Thomas Traherne and inspired or dictated these lines?

> *An object, if it were before*
> *My eye, was by Dame Nature's Law,*
> *Within my soul. Her store*
> *Was all at once within me; all her treasures*
> *Were my immediate and internal pleasures,*
> *Substantial joys, which did inform my mind.*
> *With all she wrought,*
> *My soul was fraught,*
> *And every object in my heart a thought*
> *Begot or was; I could not tell,*
> *Whether the things did there*
> *Themselves appear,*
> *Which in my spirit truly seemed to dwell;*
> *Or whether my conforming mind*
> *Were not even all that therein shined.*[36]

Later he addresses man's 'Wondrous Self':

> *O what a World art thou! A World within!*
> *All things appear,*
> *All objects are*
> *Alive in thee! Supersubstantial, rare,*
> *Above themselves, and nigh of kin*
> *To those pure things we find*
> *In His Great Mind*
> *Who made the World!*[37]

In an address to 'Thoughts', which he describes as 'brisk, divine and living things', and 'engines of Felicitie', he exclaims:

> *What were the Sky,*
> *What were the Sun, or Stars, did ye not lie*
> *In me! and represent them there*
> *Where else they never could appear!*[38]

In common with even the most convinced disciple of Berkeley, Traherne has to write and act as if the world outside himself were what it seems to be; possessed of an independent and objective existence. Doubtless this is what he really believed. For example, in *The Circulation*, he gives a list of immaterial entities—sigh, word, colour, sparkle, an influence, virtue—and points out that they must

> *borrow matter first,*
> *Before they can communicate.*

This is obvious to the simplest intelligence, if these *entia* are conceivable apart from matter. But are they so conceivable? Evidently it did not occur to Traherne to regard them as the creations of mind and matter jointly. He sees them rather as disembodied spirits, standing by to seize upon some portion of matter through which to manifest themselves, and this, he continues,

> *doth show that we must some Estate*
> *Possess, or never can communicate.*

With that objective world and himself he perceives a kind of identity which fascinates him; his relation to it is a sort of transcendent-immanence. He is one with it and yet its Lord. He and it are products of God's creative act; yet it is God's gift to him. *Thou hast put all things under his feet.* Is he in this world, or is this world in him? Both, obviously.

Circumstance will determine which is the view right for any given moment and the one that will put our personal or private universe in order. This dual relation between the world and himself inspires some of Traherne's finest poetry.

> *The World was more in me than I in it.*
> *The King of Glory in my Soul did sit.*
> *And to Himself in me He always gave,*
> *All that He takes delight to see me have.*
> *For so my Spirit was an Endless Sphere,*
> *Like God Himself, and Heaven and Earth was* [sic] *there.*[39]

Traherne sees himself so fashioned that Space and Time are annihilated. 'All my mind', he says,

> *was wholly everywhere;*
> *Whate'er it saw, 't was ever wholly there;*
> *The Sun ten thousand legions* [sic] *off, was nigh:*
> *The utmost star,*
> *Though seen from far,*
> *Was present in the apple of my eye.*
> *There was my Sight, my Life, my Sense,*
> *My Substance and my Mind.*
> *My Spirit shined*
> *Even there, not by a transient influence.*
> *The Act was immanent, yet there.*
> *The Thing remote, yet felt even here.*[40]

Traherne is merely describing in rhetorical language certain commonplaces of human existence: the power, (*a*) to apprehend distant objects through the sense organs, and thus to counteract the separation which occurs in Space; (*b*) to apprehend past events by means of memory and thus to counteract the separation which occurs in Time. Quite commonplace! Yes! But none the less *wonderful*! It is that sense of wonder at the normal activities of the human mind that Thomas Traherne seeks to awaken and he returns to the topic again and again with almost wearisome iteration. That God should so have fashioned Man that he can compass and hold in his mind

>*the great globe itself,*
>*Yea, all which it inherit,*[41]

and

>*the dark backward and abysm of time,*[42]

is more to be marvelled at than the primal act of creation itself.

> *To bring the moisture of far distant seas*
> *Into a point, to make them present here,*
> *In virtue, not in bulk; one man to please*
> *With all the powers of the highest Sphere,*
>   *From east, from west, from north and south, to bring*
> *The pleasing influence of everything;*
>
> *Is far more great than to create them there*
> *Where now they stand; His Wisdom more doth shine*
> *In that, His Might and Goodness more appear,*
> *In recollecting; He is more Divine*
>   *In making everything a gift to one*
>   *Than in the several parts of His wide Throne.*[43]

Traherne does not, however, regard Space and Time as data for a metaphysical tractate. As we have previously noted, the dry bones of pure thought have only a passing fascination for him, nor is he

> *one that would peep and botanize*
> *Upon his mother's grave.*[44]

Rather is he of that immortal company that Robert Bridges had in mind when, in his *Testament of Beauty*, he wrote:

> *What kenneth she [Science]*
> *of colour or sound? Nothing: tho' science measure true*
> *every wave-length of ether or air that reacheth sense,*
> *there the hunt checketh, and her keen hounds are at fault;*
> *for when the waves hav [sic] pass'd the gates of ear and eye*
> *all scent is lost: suddenly escaped the visibles*
> *are changed to invisible: the fine-measured motions*
> *to immeasurable emotion: the cypher'd fractions*
> *to a living joy that man feeleth to shrive his soul—*[45]

the man who knows that he lives among imponderable things! That 'living joy' was both theme and inspiration of Traherne's song, and it was nurtured in that unplumbed residuum that abides when Science shall have done her perfect work. The spirit of Bridges would have wakened instant response in his spirit had he been able to cast himself forward in time and read:

> *that there is beauty in natur [sic] and that man loveth it are one thing and the same,*[46]

for Traherne not only dallies with the idea that the reality of the objective world lies wholly in its apprehension by Mind, but, with greater plausibility, extends it to the world of the Imponderables, going so far as to suggest that this is true of the Divine attributes themselves, for

> *neither Goodness, Wisdom, Power nor Love,*
> *Nor Happiness it self in things could be,*
> *Did not they all in one fair order move,*
> *And jointly by their service end in me.*[47]

Thought, then, is an activity, and in the *Meditations* he insists that it be controlled: 'As nothing is more easy than to think, so nothing is more difficult than to think well. . . . To think well is to serve God in the interior court.'[48] This is the activity which brings near all distant things and concentrates all Time into one comprehensive NOW.

> *As in a mirror clear,*
> *Old objects I*
> *Far distant do even now descry,*
> *Which by your help are present here.*[49]

Thought is, indeed, a kind of grand precipitate of the constitution and activities of the Universe,

> *Annihilating all that's made*
> *To a green thought in a green shade.*[50]

Probably Traherne's tentative approach to Subjective Idealism is no more than an exaggerated emphasis upon the importance of Thought. Certainly the intellectual currents of the day, both here and abroad, were sweeping in the direction of such emphasis. There was, for example, his contemporary and senior by twelve years, who, like himself, just failed to reach the age of forty, Blaise Pascal (1623–62). Familiar as they must be to most readers, these noble words of his will bear repetition:

L'homme n'est qu'un roseau, le plus faible de la nature, mais c'est *un roseau pensant*. Il ne faut pas que l'univers entier s'arme pour l'écraser. Une vapeur, une goutte d'eau, suffit pour le tuer. Mais quand l'univers l'écraseroit, l'homme seroit encore plus noble que ce qui le tue, parce qu'il sait qu'il meurt; et l'avantage que l'univers a sur lui, l'univers n'en sait rien.

Toute notre dignité consiste donc en la pensée. C'est de là qu'il faut nous relever, non de l'espace et de la durée que nous ne saurions remplir. *Travaillons donc à bien penser:* voilà le principe de la morale.[51]

How well this accords with Traherne's ideas is still more apparent when we read his four poems, *Thoughts*, containing such lines as:

> *O ye conceptions of delight!*
> *Ye that inform my soul with Life and Sight!*
> *Ye representatives, and springs*
> *Of inward pleasure!*
> *Ye joys! Ye ends of outward treasure!*
> *Ye inward and ye living things!*

> *The Thought, or joy conceived is*
> *The inward fabric of my standing bliss.*
> *It is the substance of my Mind*
> *Transformed, and with its objects lined.*
> *The quintessence, elixir, spirit, cream.*
> *'Tis strange that things unseen should be supreme.*[52]

Moreover, this 'living world' of Thought is immortal:

> *It is a spiritual world within.*
> *A* Living World, *and nearer far of kin*
> *To God, than that which first He made.*
> *While that doth fade,*
> *This therefore ever shall endure,*
> *Within the soul as more divine and pure.*[53]

With increasing fervour he glorifies this power and kindles as he writes:

> *All Wisdom in a Thought doth shine,*
> *By thoughts alone the soul is made divine.*

From thoughts flow Rule, Government, and Kingdoms,

> *and so doth all the New Jerusalem.*

> *Thoughts are the things wherewith even God is crowned.*

> *A Thought*
> *Is even the very Cream of all He wrought.*

> *Thoughts are the highest things,*
> *The very Offspring of the King of Kings.*

> *A Thought can clothe itself with all the treasures*
> *Of God, and be the greatest of His Pleasures.*

> *Thoughts are things,*
> *Which rightly used make His creatures kings.*[54]

These poems on *Thought* should be read; they are pure Traherne. Their language is rich, lavish, and, some would say, extravagant and redundant. One feels the general truth of them, but they lack the precision of ordered thought and must be distressing to the mind that expects of poetry, on these themes, the measured sequence of a philosophical treatise. It is when we take them as a whole and are content with general impressions that they make their strongest appeal. When we begin to examine them clause by clause the questions raised have a sobering effect upon our earlier appreciation. 'What does he *really* mean?' we ask again and again, and echo answers: 'What?' Nevertheless, whether we can or cannot accept and enter into the meaning of his every glowing phrase and flight of fancy, he reinvigorates for us the familiar words of Edward Dyer, who died thirty years before Traherne was born, and gratefully we make them our own again:

> *My mind to me a kingdom is,*
> *Such perfect joy therein I find,*
> *That it excels all other bliss*
> *That world affords or grows by kind;*
> *Though much I want which most would have,*
> *Yet still my mind forbids to crave.* [55]

Traherne advances the speculation that the supreme pleasure of God lies in beholding the happiness of men: that happiness which has been created by this power of thought: the interplay between the human mind and the objective world. He treads dizzy heights in his mystic's progress:

> *Happiness is His delight,*
> *His creatures' happiness as well as His:*
> *For that in truth He seeks, and 'tis His Bliss.* [56]

Nor does his probing mind rest at this point, but professes to see the worth of all things solely in their worth for mankind. It is temerarious speculation, only finally to be justified on the assumption that Mind alone has true existence. That once granted, Traherne's estimate of values would seem to follow as a matter of course. Value would then be of the same order of existence as the Divine attributes. As we should expect, he goes on to declare that it is only their value for man that causes objects to have value for God:

> *The Godhead cannot prize*
> *The Sun at all, nor yet the Skies,*
> *Or Air, or Earth, or Trees, or Seas,*
> *Or Stars, unless the soul of man they please.*
>
> *The joy and pleasure which His Soul doth take*
> *In all His works, is for His creatures' sake.*
> *So great a certainty*
> *We in this holy doctrine see,*
> *That there could be no worth at all*
> *In any thing material, great or small,*
> *Were not some Creature more alive,*
> *Whence it might worth derive.*
> *God is the spring whence things came forth;*
> *Souls are the fountains of their real worth.*
>
> *The joy and pleasure which His soul doth take*
> *In all His works, is for His creatures' sake.*
> *Yet doth He take delight*
> *That's altogether infinite*
> *In them, even as they from Him come;*
> *For such His love and goodness is, the sum*
> *Of all His happiness doth seem,*
> *At least in His esteem,*
> *In that delight and joy to lie,*
> *Which is His blessed creatures' Melody.*
>
> *In them He sees, and feels, and smells, and lives,*
> *By them affected is to whom He gives:*
> *In them ten thousand ways,*
> *He all His works again enjoys,*
> *All things from Him to Him proceed*
> *By them; are His in them.*[57]

Has he made God and Man identical? It is difficult to say, but he has certainly come very near to it: nor does his fancy stay there. So great is man's power over the objective world, so dependent is it upon him for any value that it may possess, that he himself enhances its value in the very act of enjoying it, and so makes it more acceptable to God.

> *His gifts as they to us come down*
> *Are infinite, and crown*
> *The soul with strange fruitions; yet*
> *Returning from us they more value get.* [58]

Again:

> *That we should make the skies*
> *More glorious far before Thine eyes*
> *Than Thou didst make them, and even Thee*
> *Far more Thy works prize,*
> *As used they be,*
> *Than as they're made; is a stupendous work,*
> *Wherein Thy wisdom mightily doth lurk.* [59]

In all these speculations about the relations between God and Man Traherne shows affinity with the tortured, questing element in the thought of ancient Greece, as represented in such a work as the *Prometheus Bound* of Æschylus. This is expressed in an eloquent and illuminating passage by Professor W. Macneile Dixon, in his book, *Tragedy*. He is writing of the *Prometheus* (the italics are mine):

It supposes gods and men partners in an enterprise of which neither foresees the end, and the secret of Prometheus, if rendered into modern terms, might serve as an allegory for the knowledge that man is as necessary to Zeus as he to man: *since without him nature would want spectators, and be in fact nothing, as though it were not.* To his consciousness nature is in debt, to him she appears, *through his eye and mind alone perceives herself and thus comes into full and true existence. He receives from nature a body, he gives in exchange a soul.* Without him the kingdom of Zeus is, *if so much*, at most a material kingdom, an empty shell, an unilluminated void, *an unperceived gyration*, a senseless dust. *Lifted out of apparent insignificance, man thus becomes and is in simple fact, a necessary pillar of the universe.* To give nature a meaning, a higher value, a soul, in the magnitude of such an undertaking lies, perhaps, his privilege and—his tragedy.[60]

These words, had it been Traherne's good fortune to read them, must have come to him as sunshine into a clouded sky, as the opening of a door into a darkened room. Would he not have exclaimed, 'I, too, wished to say these things, but my thought became entangled in the verbiage of its way'?

The theologically minded reader is sure in course of time to ask, 'What about Sin? Does it appear in all this somewhat fantastic scheme of things, this medley of human and divine, and, if so, how?' In these *Poems,* as distinct from the *Meditations,* it figures very little. Like Crashaw, Traherne seems to have been barely troubled by it. Certainly he was no *Mea Culpa* man, which a certain type of piety will note to his discredit. He sees how 'filthy sin' destroys the sweetness of life and takes a line of his own by tracing its beginnings to the acquirement of the power of speech. His theory is that man's life begins and continues for some time in a state of speechlessness, which is a beneficent design on the part of God, to the end that the soul may have a space to

> *meditate on things,*
> *And to contemplate the eternal springs*
> *Of God and Nature, Glory, Bliss, and Pleasure;*
> *That Life and Love might be his heavenly treasure:*
> *And therefore speechless made at first, that he*
> *Might in himself profoundly busied be:*
> *And not vent out, before he hath t'en in*
> *Those antidotes that guard his soul from sin.*[61]

To what extent the infant mind is capable of engaging in such profound occupations we must leave to our psychologists to determine. Hence he is not

> *depraved with tongues,*
> *Nor injured by the errors and the wrongs*
> *That* mortal words *convey.*

He assures us, his 'Dear friends', that this was his own 'blessed case':

> *For nothing spoke to me but the fair face*
> *Of heaven and earth, before myself could speak,*
> I then my bliss did, when my silence, break.

'Is this', we ask, 'memory or imagination?' If the former, Traherne must have been an extraordinary child. He asserts that he was

> *pent within*
> *A fort, impregnable to any sin:*
> *Till the avenues being open laid,*
> *Whole legions entered, and the forts betrayed.*

During the silent period he had found

> *every Stone, and every Star a tongue,*
> *And every Gale of Wind a curious song.*
> *The heavens were an oracle, and spake*
> Divinity: *the Earth did undertake*
> *The office of a Priest; and I being dumb*
> (*Nothing besides was dumb*) *all things did come*
> *With voices and instructions;* but when I
> Had gained a tongue, their power began to die.
> *Mine ears let other noises in, not theirs;*
> *A noise disturbing all my songs and prayers.*
> *My foes pulled down the Temple to the ground,*
> *They my adoring soul did deeply wound.*[62]

It is beautifully, poignantly said and has the ring of truth, though not all the truth. His diatribe should be, not against speech in itself, but against the wicked and foolish uses that men make of it. He failed to realize how interdependent are the powers of speech and thought, and how he was weakening his own exalted doctrine of Thought in disregarding the extent to which it is a product of Speech. Shelley was amongst those who have been aware of this vital connexion.

One of the many blessings that his *Prometheus* bestowed upon man was that

> *He gave man speech, and speech created thought,*
> *Which is the measure of the universe.*[63]

With the last statement Traherne would have heartily agreed, but the truth of the first line appears to have escaped him.

Nevertheless, however life may have dealt with him after speech had invaded his solitude, he is sure that there is a precious something that remains, the fruit of those early, meditative years.

> *Yet the first words mine infancy did hear,*
> *The things which in my dumbness did appear,*
> *Preventing all the rest, got such a root*
> *Within my heart, and stick so close unto't*
> *It may be trampled on, but still will grow;*
> *And nutriment to soil itself will owe.*
> *The first impressions are immortal all.*
> *And let mine enemies whoop, cry, roar, or call,*
> *Yet these will whisper if I will but hear,*
> *And penetrate the heart, if not the ear.*[64]

So, with Wordsworth, he believed that

> *those first affections,*
> *Those shadowy recollections,*
> *Which, be they what they may,*
> *Are yet the fountain-light of all our day,*
> *Are yet a master-light of all our seeing;*
> *Uphold us, cherish, and have power to make*
> *Our noisy years seem moments in the being*
> *Of the eternal Silence: truths that wake*
> *To perish never:*
> *Which neither listlessness, nor mad endeavour,*
> *Nor Man nor Boy,*
> *Nor all that is at enmity with joy,*
> *Can utterly abolish or destroy.*[65]

In accordance with the prevalent religious ideas of the age Traherne associates this early period of infancy with the state of the unfallen Adam, which was generally regarded as the ideal state of existence, and those who extolled it seemed incapable of realizing its manifest and manifold limitations. His own early years he envisages as being of that order.

> *Only what Adam in his first estate,*
>   *Did I behold;*
>   *Hard silver and dry gold*
> *As yet lay under ground; my blessed fate*
>   *Was more acquainted with the old*
> *And innocent delights, which he did see*
> *In his original simplicity.*
>
> *Those things which first his Eden did adorn,*
>   *My infancy*
>   *Did crown.*[66]
>
>   *I was an Adam there,*
> *A little Adam in a sphere*
> *Of joys.*[67]
>
> *All bliss*
> *Consists in this,*
> *To do as Adam did.*[68]

God's goodness being so great in the creation of man's joy, Traherne asks:

> *Am I a glorious spring*
> *Of joys and riches to my King?*[69]

This is a personal question, quite distinct from his general thesis that God desires to find His own joy in that of His creatures. In general terms,

> *To see us but receive, is such a sight*
> *As makes His treasures infinite;*
> *Because His Goodness doth possess*
> *In us, His own, and our own blessedness.*

But there are irresponsive creatures, who bring sorrow instead of joy to the Divine heart.

> *If we despise His glorious works,*
> *Such sin and mischief in it lurks,*
> *That they are all made vain,*
> *And this is even endless pain*
> *To Him that sees it. Whose diviner grief*
> *Is hereupon (Ah me!) without relief.*
> *We please His goodness that receive:*
> *Refusers Him of all bereave.*

It is our love that God wants and nothing else will satisfy Him.

> *All gold and silver is but empty dross;*
> *Rubies and sapphires are but loss;*
> *The very Sun and Stars and Seas*
> *Far less His Spirit please.*
> *One voluntary act of love*
> *Far more delightful to His Soul doth prove,*
> *And is above all these as far as Love.*[70]

So Traherne descends a little from his heights of mysticism to levels where the ordinary mind can follow and understand. He is a disciple, at any rate for a few moments, of St. John of the New Testament, and the man who falters before Traherne's somewhat incoherent metaphysics may respond to his plea to answer, with his own love and devotion, the infinite love of God, for

> *The Face of God is Goodness unto all.*[71]

There is, in the *Poems*, the outline of a doctrine of God, but it is many-sided and lacking in lucidity. Traherne's concern with God is equally a concern with Man; each exists for the other. They are almost correlates: so much so that, as we have noted, there are times when his mysticism approaches identification. On occasion there is a pantheistic tendency that almost equates God with Nature. Sometimes he writes of God as incarnate in Humanity; a truth, but one which needs to be circumspectly expressed. The reverent modern mind would shrink from such a statement as

In them [His creatures] He sees, and feels, and smells, and lives.[72]

This is crude, and more than anthropomorphic, or descriptive of the nature and activities of God in terms applicable only to human beings. He attributes the human activities themselves to God. In what he calls the 'endlessness' of God's works, he sees evidence that God is 'in all divine—a DEITY', a curious and unnecessary comment if words have a recognizable meaning. What would be the status of a 'God' who was neither 'in all divine', nor a 'deity'? This God, alone, is self-sufficing:

> *Only 'tis God above,*
> *That from, and in Himself doth live.*[73]

In the poem entitled *The Anticipation* Traherne comes to a closer consideration of a doctrine of God, and certain of his words and expressions show the influence of Scholasticism: e.g. End, Means, Cause, Efficient. God is the Beginning and the End of His own Creation: that is, all creatures have their origin in Him and their purpose is to find in Him the end or goal of their being, with the perfect satisfaction which that brings. That is good theology, but not distinctively Christian. Beginning and End have alike existed in God 'from everlasting':

> *Both are the very same.*
> *The End and Fountain differ but in name.*

So Traherne arrives at a conception of 'the Eternal Now':

> *His Name is NOW, His Nature is For ever.*

Since

> *the means whereby God is, must perfect be,*
> *God is Himself the means*
> *Whereby He doth exist.*[74]

The whole discussion approaches the level of the familiar question of childhood: 'Where did God come from?' There is an air of profundity about Traherne's words but in reality they neither tell us anything nor lead us anywhere.

Whether or not, like his famous contemporary Spinoza, he was aware of the philosophical difficulties of the position, he quite definitely attributes Desire to God, on the ground that without it Joy is impossible, Joy being the gratification of Desire. In these words he sings its praise:

> *Wants are the fountains of Felicitie.*
> >   *No joy could ever be*
> >   *Were there no Want. No bliss,*
> *No sweetness perfect were it not for this.*
> >   *Want is the greatest pleasure*
> >   *Because it makes all treasure.*
> *O what a wonderful, profound abyss*
> *Is God! In whom eternal wants and treasures*
> *Are more delightful 'cause they both are pleasures.*
>
> *He infinitely wanteth all his joys;*
> >   *And all those wanted pleasures*
> *He infinitely hath.*

Further, God's 'Essence is all Act', an Act that communicates itself, and

> *From all to all eternity He is*
> *That Act; an Act of bliss.*
>
> *And Holy, Holy, Holy is His Name.*[78]

This Theism is attractively musical as Traherne sets it forth, though the rhyming of 'treasures' and 'pleasures' becomes wearisome; but it is sketchy, highly 'mystical', and lacking in clarity. Yet the sincerity of the man who wrote it is beyond question and perhaps his ideas were clearer to himself than he has been able to make them to his readers. He is never sufficiently explicit for us to regard him as a man with strong convictions in matters metaphysical. He does not linger over or develop his thought, but passes like a butterfly from flower to flower, returning to each again and again and again, to sip the same brand of nectar. The result is bewildering, as we have seen more than once: subjective and objective views, not only of Nature, but of God, jostling each other on the same page. In part extenuation we should remember that Traherne was a poet rather than a philosopher, and so make allowance for moods and impulses and refrain from pressing our questions with embarrassing insistence.

These poems, deeply religious as they are, are by no means a running commentary on the beliefs of the Church of which their author was a minister. It is to *Centuries of Meditations* that we must turn for distinctively Christian doctrine, where we find it well balanced with Traherne's naturalism. The *Poems* are naturalistic and theistic, but no mere Theist ever expressed more fervent joy or experienced richer intimacy with God. If this is Theism only, it is Theism in the matrix of the Christian Revelation. Toward the end of the Dobell Manuscript a few ideas distinctively Christian make a cursory and rather timid appearance:

> *And all the glory of His Passion prize,*
> *Who for thee lives, who for thee dies.*[76]

> *Jesu's blood refines the soul from sin.*
> *His grievous Cross is a supreme delight,*
> *And of all heavenly ones the greatest sight.*—[77]

which is very anæmic stuff beside such robust and soaring lines as John Wesley's

> *While Jesu's blood through earth and skies*
> *Mercy, free, boundless mercy! cries.*[78]

We miss, though not necessarily with regret, those pivots around which George Herbert's poetry moves: Church festivals, Church ritual, Church buildings, and the terminology of ancient confessions of Faith. Has Thomas Traherne failed to discern the values in these things, or is he one of those rare spirits who have passed beyond them? As objects of thought they must have been familiar to him, for he was an ordained clergyman of the Church of England, but when he was writing these poems he seems to have sat very loosely to them and hardly do they appear to have been fundamental in his spiritual life. Perhaps he was aware of them as a traveller is aware of the beauty of the Swiss valley through which he is passing, but whose imagination and desire are toward the snow-clad mountain peaks ahead. Or perhaps he had entered so far into the New Jerusalem that he could say with assurance and without regret: *I saw no Temple therein: for the Lord God the Almighty, and the Lamb, are the Temple thereof.*[79] If so, he walked in such heavenly altitudes as George Herbert had not reached when he chose, as a descriptive title for his poems, *The Temple*. Herbert was of the devout company of those who linger in the Palace Beautiful; Thomas Traherne was rather of those who have seen from the upper windows of the Palace the Delectable Mountains and 'bethink themselves of setting forward'.

Sir A. Quiller-Couch refers to Traherne as 'an exceedingly humble man at heart'; 'a humble Welsh parson'; 'a poor Welsh parson'. Poor in worldly estate he certainly was, as is evidenced by the few and rather pathetic bequests in his hastily made will; but spiritually he was rich. He could have sung, full-throated, those lines of Charles Wesley, which would make an average Church congregation of today shudder:

> *On all the kings of earth*
> *With pity we look down;*
> *And claim in virtue of our birth,*
> *A never fading crown.*[80]

The supreme, inescapable fact about him is that he is a rejoicing, buoyantly happy Christian, who, like the rest of us, has his moments of lesser exaltation. In all his twists and turns of fancy we may be unable to follow him, but he has the thing that matters—JOY; joy that sings and soars: and he wants us to share it with him. 'Enter thou into my Joy' is his urgent invitation, and as we read there is something in us that must respond. He acknowledges that he himself had slighted the Divine call, and the wonder of God's love had been declared in this,

> *that Thou*
> *Thyself should'st me convert, I scarce know how.*

Like Enoch he 'walked with God':

> *He did approach, He me did woo;*
> *I wonder that my God this thing would do.*[81]

Of the great hymn-writers of the following century he has closer affinity with Isaac Watts, in his God-in-Creation mood, than with Charles Wesley, in whom the mood is rare. When Watts exhorts us,

> *Praise ye the Lord! 'tis good to raise*
> *Our hearts and voices in His praise;*
> *His nature and His works invite*
> *To make this duty our delight,*

Traherne's soul, could he have heard, would have responded gleefully, for his was a riotously anti-Barthian delight that saw God in every lovely thing.

> *In all His works, in all His ways,*
> *We must His glory see and praise.*[82]

A happy man, singing out his heart's joyance because he must: singing it for sheer gladness at the meaning and music of it all! To him it is the ever-recurring miracle of life and the wonder of it is endlessly renewed in his soul and in his song.

> *These things who knows,*
> *With Joy and Praise he goes.*[83]

Notes and References

I. Religion under the Stars. Henry Vaughan

QUOTATIONS are from *Sacred Poems and Pious Ejaculations*, by Henry Vaughan, 'Silurist', with a Memoir by the Rev. H. F. Lyte; published in the *Aldine Edition* by Geo. Bell & Sons, 1891. With few exceptions, I have retained the spelling of this edition.

Vaughan and Herbert. Readers interested in Herbert's influence upon Vaughan should consult a charming little edition of Vaughan's *Silex Scintillans*, published by the Gresham Publishing Co., with an Introduction by W. A. Lewis Bettany. In fifty pages of the Appendix there is set out what the compiler wisely calls 'parallel passages' rather than plagiarisms.

1. Izaak Walton: *Life of Mr. George Herbert.*
2. See note above.
3. Chaucer: *Prologue to Canterbury Tales*, line 527.
4. Tennyson: *In Memoriam*, xcvi.
5. *Repentance.*
6. Marlowe: *Tragical History of Doctor Faustus.* Quarto, 1604.
7. *Abel's Blood.*
8. *Easter Hymn.*
9. *Misery.*
10. *Palm-Sunday.*
11. Romans viii. 21.
12. *Love-Sick.*
13. (*a*) *Poetical Works of John and Charles Wesley*, Vol. V, 137. (*b*) *A Collection of Hymns for the Use of the People Called Methodists* [1779], 428.

    Note. Hereafter these will be referred to as (*a*) *P.W.*; (*b*) *Hymns* [1779.]

14. *P.W.*, Vol. II, 92. *Hymns* [1779], 105.
15. *The Timber.*
16. *Misery.*
17. *Dressing.*
18. *The Men of War.*
19. Coleridge: *Frost at Midnight*, line 65.

20. Edwyn Bevan: *Symbolism and Belief*, p. 278.
21. W. H. Davies: *The Happy Child*.
22. *The Constellation*.
23. John Keats: Sonnet: '*When I have fears* . . .'
24. Sir Henry Wotton: *On His Mistress, the Queen of Bohemia*.
25. Swinburne: *At a Month's End*.
26. *Stars*.
27. *Ibid*.
28. Psalm cxxxix. 11 and 12 (R.V. margin).
29. George Meredith: *Hymn to Colour*.
30. *Departed Friends*.
31. *Peace*.
32. *Resurrection and Immortality*.

II. A Mystic in Half-lights. Francis Quarles

Quotations are from *Emblems, Divine and Moral*: By Francis Quarles. Published by Wm. Paterson, Edinburgh, 1888. The spelling of this Edition is modern.

The alleged humour of Quarles. F. E. Hutchinson, writing on Quarles in the Cambridge History of English Literature, Vol. VII, p. 47, refers to his 'rough humour'. I doubt, however, if Quarles *intended* to be humorous. If he did, he failed: at any rate, to an age like our own. Take, for example, his reference to 'dunghill worldlings, you that root like swine', and his descriptions of a game of bowls and of tobacco. If he *meant* to be 'funny', the humour is too heavy-footed for a generation nurtured on *Punch*, and he barely provokes a smile. If, however, he was *serious*, as I like to think he was, the smiles broaden and turn to laughter, not so much at what he said as at the seriousness of Quarles himself on such subjects, *expressed in such a way*. There is much in Quarles that gives us keener pleasure if we regard him as serious rather than humorous, but it is not always the kind of pleasure that he intended.

1. *Letters of John Wesley* (Standard Edition, 8 Vols.), Vol. III, p. 334.

> [*Note*. All references to John Wesley's *Letters* and *Journal* are to the Standard Editions, published by the Epworth Press.]
> [Jacob Behmen, Boehme, Böhme or Böhm (all these spellings occur in English books), 1575–1624, was a shoemaker of Görlitz, a theosophist and a mystic, who influenced both Henry More (see Study V) and William Law. See Ueberweg's *History of Philosophy*, Vol. II, p. 29. There is an admirable short account of him and an analysis of his teaching in Schwegler's *History of Philosophy*, pp. 153–6.]

2. *Emblems.* I, 9.
3. II, xi (Epigram).
4. II, viii.
5. IV, xiv.
6. V, xi.
7. V, xv.
8. IV, xiv.
9. I, ii.
10. I, i.
11. I, ii.
12. *Paradise Lost,* Book IX, line 782.
13. I, Invocation.
14. *P.W.*, Vol. V, p. 480 [1779], 16.
15. Tibullus. I, iii, 47 and 35, I suggest:
    Then were there no embattled hosts, nor enmity nor wars; neither did the sword-smith ply his ungentle craft.
  and,
    What bliss it was to live when Saturn ruled!
16. *King Richard II,* II, i, 42.
17. I. ii.
18. I, v.
19. G. K. Chesterton: *Watts,* p. 109.
20. II, v.
21. I, xiv.
22. See *History of Kingswood School,* by Three Old Boys. pp. 26 and 79.
23. I, x.
24. II, iv.
25. *I King Henry IV,* V, i.
26. Emerson: Essay on *Self-reliance.*
27. 1 Corinthians xiii.
28. V, vi.
29. Wm. Combe: *Doctor Syntax: A Tour in Search of the Picturesque.* Canto xiv.
30. Lewis Carroll: *Alice Through the Looking-glass.*
31. Matthew vi. 26.
32. *As You Like It,* II, v, 1.
33. Thomas Nashe: *Spring.*
34. John Donne: *Elegie on Mrs. Boulstred.*
35. V, xii.
36. *Paradise Lost,* IV, 343.
37. III, viii.
38. Psalm viii. 4 and 5.
39. III, v.

40. *Hymns* [1779], 182.
41. Christina Rossetti: *For Thine Own Sake, O my God.*
42. V, iv.
43. III, x.
44. *Hymns* [1779], 33.
45. W. H. Davies: *The Dreaming Boy.*
46. *King John*, III, iv, 93.
47. IV, ix. Quarles actually has 'springs' for 'arms'.
48. Euripides: *Medea.* Translation by Sir Gilbert Murray, p. 61.
49. III, vii. *Methodist Hymn-book* (1933), 162.
50. Milton: *L'Allegro.*

III. *Cross and Crucifix. Richard Crashaw*

Quotations are from *The English Poems of Richard Crashaw*, edited by Edward Hutton and published in the *Little Library* by Methuen & Co., 1901.

There is a handy edition in *The Muses' Library*, published by Geo. Routledge & Sons, with notes and various readings by J. R. Tutin and an Introduction by Canon Beeching. It also contains posthumous poems not included in the first-mentioned edition.

The *Complete Works*, including the Latin Poems, may be found in *The Library of Old Authors*, published by John Russell Smith, Soho Square, in 1858, and edited by Wm. B. Turnbull.

In all these editions the spelling has been largely modernized.

1. Abraham Cowley: *On the Death of Mr. Crashaw.*
2. *St. Mary Magdalene*, XX.
3. *The Epiphany of our Lord.*
4. See *Mr. Pope*, by Geo. Paston, Vol. II, p. 37; also *The Muses' Library* edition of Crashaw's Poems (see above), pp. li and lii.
5. *Office of Holy Cross.*
6. Dante: *Inferno*, II, 23.

> *lo loco santo,*
> *u'siede il successor del maggior Piero.*

7. The *Little Library* edition of Crashaw's Poems, p. xiii.
8. Juvenal: *Satire*, iii, 183–4. As translation should be of *meaning* rather than *words*, I suggest: *In Rome, one must 'pay through the nose' for everything.*
9. Francis Thompson: *Envoy.*
10. *Julius Caesar*, III, i, 200 and 259.
11. *On the Wounds of Our Crucified Lord.*
12. *Divine Epigrams.*

13. Milton: *Il Penseroso*.
14. John Donne: *Goodfriday, 1613. Riding Westward*.
15. *Sancta Maria Dolorum*.
16. Walter de la Mare: *They Told Me* (*Collected Poems*, p. 125).
17. *Ibid., Clear Eyes* (*Ibid.*, p. 251).
18. *Saint Joan*, Scene vi.
19. The *Madman* in John Masefield's *Good Friday*.
20. *Sancta Maria Dolorum*, vii.
21. Charles Wesley: *Hymns on the Lord's Supper* (1745), No. 22. *P.W.*, Vol. III, p. 232.
22. *The Hymn of St. Thomas*.
23. Dante: *Paradiso*, xxv.
    Questi è colui che giacque sopra 'l petto
    del nostro pellicano. . . .
24. Hymns [1779], 337. *Methodist Hymn-book* (1933), 456.
25. *Ibid.*, 124. *Ibid.*, 172.
26. *Ibid.*, 194. *Ibid.*, 368.
27. *Ibid.*, 32. *Ibid.*, 173.
28. *P.W.*, Vol. IX, 362. *Hymns* (1933), 457.
29. *P.W.*, Vol. VI, p. 143. *Hymns* (1933), 264.
30. Colossians ii. 14.
31. *Sancta Maria Dolorum*.
32. Sir A. Quiller-Couch: *Studies in Literature*, I. 'Some Seventeenth-century Poets.'
33. *Paradise Lost*, III, 410.
34. *To the Name above every Name, the Name of Jesus*.
35. *Methodist Hymn-book* (1933), 179.
36. *Against Irresolution and Delay in Matters of Religion*.
37. Virgil: *Eclogue*, I, 7.
38. Keats: *Ode to a Nightingale*.
39. Robert Burns: *Highland Mary*.
40. Alexander Whyte: *Santa Teresa*, pp. 10 and 11.
41. Coleridge: *Additional Table Talk* (Bohn, p. 322).
42. *Paradise Lost*, VII, 205.
43. Wordsworth: *Sonnet to Milton*, Oxford Poets, p. 307.
44. *Prayer*, Part II.
45. *Description of a Religious House*.

IV. The Scrutiny of the Soul. Sir John Davies

Quotations are from *The Complete Poems of Sir John Davies*, edited by Alex. B. Grosart, in the *Early English Poets* series, and published in two volumes by Chatto and Windus, in 1876.

The sequence of the quotations is almost the same as in the text of the poem—*Of the Soule of Man and the Immortalite Thereof*—and references are not given. Except by noting the pages of some particular edition, this would not be easy, as the stanzas are not numbered.

1. Coleridge: *Kubla Khan*, line 30.
2. Xenophon: *Cyropaedia*, Book VIII, 13.
3. *King Lear*, I, ii, 132.
4. Book of Common Prayer, Second Prayer of the Litany.
5. Tennyson: *Idylls of the King; Guinevere*.
6. Quotations follow from the First Part of the poem: *Of Humane Knowledge*.
7. *Works of John Wesley* (Ed. 1872), Vol. VII, p. 342.
8. Plato: *Protagoras*, 343.
9. Juvenal: *Satire*, xi, 27.
10. Robert Bridges: *The Testament of Beauty*, Book IV, 767.
11. Charles Dickens: *Nicholas Nickleby*, Chapter XII.
12. Walt Whitman: *Song of Myself*, 48.
13. *Ibid*.
14. Sir Thomas Browne: *Religio Medici*, Part II (Everyman, p. 83).
15. *Paradise Lost*, II, 62.
16. Wordsworth: *The River Duddon*, xxxiv, *After-Thought*.
17. E. M. W. Tillyard: *The Elizabethan World Picture*, pp. 5 and 6.
18. *Paradise Lost*, VIII, 122.
19. Coleridge: *Christabel*, line 52.
20. *Paradise Lost*, IV, 773.
21. Matthew Prior: *Solomon*, closing lines of Book I.
22. J. Dover Wilson: *The Essential Shakespeare*, p. 15.
23. Matthew Prior: Lines just previous to those of Note 21 (*supra*).
24. Plato: *Phaedo*, 118.
25. Xenophon: *Memorabilia of Socrates*, Book IV, ii, 24–39.
26. M. R. James: *The Apocryphal New Testament*, p. 28.
27. Quotations from this point are from *Of the Soule of Man and the Immortalite Thereof*.
28. Abbot Alcuin. See *Mediaeval Latin Lyrics*, by Helen Waddell, pp. 94–5. Her translation is:
    > Wherefore bethink thee rather of thy soul
    > Than of thy flesh; this dieth, that abides.
29. Beaumont and Fletcher: *A King and No King*, IV, iv.
30. Jeremy Taylor: *Selected Passages*, by L. Pearsall Smith, p. 183.
31. Benjamin Whichcote: *Moral and Religious Aphorisms*, No. 71.
32. *Letters of John Wesley*, Vol. IV, p. 38.
33. Plato: *Phaedrus*, 250.

34. Marcus Aurelius: X, i. Thus translated by R. W. Livingstone in *The Mission of Greece*, p. 91.
35. Edmund Waller: The conclusion of *Divine Poems*.
36. H. Vaughan: *Resurrection and Immortality*.
37. Jeremy Taylor. See *supra*, Note 30, p. 200.
38. Roger Bacon. Quoted by W. Macneile Dixon in *Tragedy*, p. 179.
39. Robt. Browning: *Apparent Failure*, final stanza.
40. Æschylus: *Agamemnon*, translation by Sir Gilbert Murray, p. 64.
41. Walter Pater: *The Renaissance: Leonardo da Vinci*.
42. *A Midsummer Night's Dream*, V. i, 10.
43. Thos. Nashe: *In Time of Pestilence*.
44. Rupert Brooke: *Menelaus and Helen*.
45. Walter de la Mare: *Mirage* (*Collected Poems*, p. 303).
46. Chris. Marlowe: *Doctor Faustus*.
47. Lucretius: *De Rerum Natura*, I, 155.
48. Berdyaev: *The Destiny of Man*, p. 163.
49. *Works of John Wesley* (1872), Vol. IX, 470.
50. Boswell's *Johnson:* June, 1784.
51. William Watson: *The Great Misgiving*.
52. *Minutes of Conference*, 1745.
53. *Works of John Wesley* (1872), Vol. VI, 141.
54. *Letters of John Wesley*, Vol. IV, 197.
55. John Donne: *Sermons*, Selected Passages (L. Pearsall Smith), p. 13.
56. *Ibid.*, p. 224.

V. A Cynic among the Sectaries. Henry More

Henry More's Works are not to be 'picked up' on 'almost any second-hand bookstall'. Far from it! I have used the rather sumptuous edition, published under the Ward Bequest by the Manchester University Press, 1931, and admirably introduced and annotated by Geoffrey Bullough. When this volume is reprinted, the Hebrew references should be revised by a competent Hebrew scholar. There are numerous misprints, most of them owing to confusion between Hebrew characters very similar in shape.

I have modernized much of the spelling and occasionally revised the punctuation. References to the quotations are not given, as their sequence is as in the poem itself.

The full title of the edition used is *Philosophical Poems of Henry More, comprising Psychozoia and Minor Poems*.

1. Shelley: *Adonais*, xxxix.
2. W. S. Gilbert: *Patience*.
3. Burnet: *History of His Own Times*, Book II.

4. W. R. Sorley: *History of English Philosophy*, pp. 75–6.
5. Quoted *ibid.*, p. 77.
6. Sir Thomas Browne: Christian Morals, Part I, xix.
7. Basil Willey: *The Seventeenth-century Background*, p. 160.
8. Robt. Browning: *The Lost Leader*.
9. Julian Huxley: *Essays of a Biologist*, Religion and Science.
10. *Romeo and Juliet*, II, ii, 43.
11. *King Henry* V, IV, i, 37.
12. Wm. Myles: *Chronological History of the People called Methodists* (3rd Ed., 1803), pp. 87–8. These questions and answers were part of the business of the Conference of 1763, held in London, of which no official *Minutes* were published.
13. John Wesley's *Journal*, iii, 170. *Letters*, ii, 34.
14. See R. W. Livingstone: *The Mission of Greece*, p. 142.
15. Plato: *Epistle iv*. In the *Timaeus* volume of the Loeb Classical Library, p. 447. The context suggests *snobbery* as a possible translation of αὐθάδεια, although Liddell and Scott give only *stubbornness, presumption* and their analogues.
16. Byron: *English Bards and Scotch Reviewers*, line 5.
17. Samuel Butler: *Hudibras*, Part I, Canto i.
18. Quoted by E. M. W. Tillyard: *The Elizabethan World Picture*, p. 68.
19. On the Sectaries, the reader should consult the *Autobiography* of Richard Baxter, e.g.:

> Had it not been for the faction of the Prelatists on one side that drew men off, and the factions of the giddy and turbulent sectaries on the other side ... England had been like in a quarter of an age to have become a land of saints and a pattern of holiness to all the world, and the unmatchable paradise of the earth. (*Everyman*, p. 84.)
>
> The poor Church of Christ, the sober, sound religious part, are like Christ that was crucified between two malefactors; the profane and formal persecutors on one hand, and the fanatic dividing sectary on the other hand, have in all ages been grinding the spiritual seed as the corn is ground between the millstones.... (*Ibid.*, p. 90.)

20. *As You Like It*, II, vii, 12.
21. T. Carlyle: *Sartor Resartus*, Book I, Chapter iv.
22. *Hamlet:* III, ii, 400.
23. *Paradise Lost*, IV, 288.
24. *Ibid.*, 323.
25. Ovid: *Metamorphoses*, Lib. III, 417.

26. Kierkegaard. Quoted by H. R. Mackintosh, *Types of Modern Theology*, p. 228.
27. Ovid. See No. 25, 504.
28. J. Donne: Sermons (L. Pearsall Smith), pp. 67-8.
29. *Paradise Lost*, IV, 456.
30. *The Pilgrim's Progress*, Part I, Chapter XII.
31. Dryden: *Absalom and Achitophel*, Book I, 534.
32. Geo. Crabbe: Tale XIV, *Struggles of Conscience*.
33. Jonathan Swift: Preface to *The Battle of the Books*.
34. W. Cowper: *The Task*, Book II, *The Timepiece*, 332.
35. *Ibid.*, 409.
36. Anthony Trollope: The Barchester Novels.
37. Dryden: *Absalom and Achitophel*, Part I, line 545, adapted. Original:
    *A man so varied that he seemed to be
    Not one, but all mankind's epitome.*
38. 1 Samuel ii. 36.
39. Quoted in Basil Willey's *Seventeenth-century Background*, p. 25.
40. Pope: *Essay on Man*, Ep. I, 17.
41. Francis Quarles: *Emblems*, II, iii.
42. Euripides: *The Bacchae*. Sir Gilbert Murray's Translation, p. 44.
43. W. R. Inge: *The Platonic Tradition in English Religious Thought*, p. 56.
44. S. T. Coleridge: *Omniana* (Bohn, p. 392).
45. *Ibid.*
46. H. More, II, 19.
47. *Ibid.*, II, 91.
48. A. N. Whitehead: *Adventures of Ideas*, Chapter XIX (p. 358).
49. Quoted in *Philosophical Poems of H. More*, Introduction, liv.
50. *Hymns* [1779], 444. [1933], 284.
51. *Hymns* [1779], 445. [1933], 301.
52. 1933, 220.
53. John Wesley's Works (1872), Vol. X, 491-2.
54. Æschylus: *Eumenides*. Translated by Sir Gilbert Murray in *The Oresteia*, p. 228. N.B. The order of the stanzas is here reversed.

VI. Songs of Spiritual 'Felicitie'. Thomas Traherne

For the serious reader of Thomas Traherne there is but one edition, *The Poetical Works of Thos. Traherne*, 1932, to which should be added the companion volume, *Centuries of Meditations*, 1927. I have modernized much of the spelling and some of the punctuation.

Again I express my very sincere thanks to the publishers and owners of the copyright, Messrs. P. J. and A. E. Dobell, for permission to make such extensive quotations.

1. Swinburne: *The Garden of Proserpine.*
2. Pope: *Imitations of Horace*, Book II, Ep. I, 72.
3. Geo. Crabbe: *The Library*, 157.
4. Eugene Field: *Wynken, Blynken and Nod.*
5. *Centuries of Meditations*, Third Century, 46.
6. Wordsworth: *Elegiac Stanzas on Peele Castle in a Storm.*
7. *The Salutation*, ii.
8. *Ibid.*, iii.
9. Thos. Browne: *Religio Medici*, Part I (Everyman, p. 64).
10. *The Salutation*, vi.
11. *Ibid.*, v.
12. Francis Darwin: *Life of Charles Darwin*, end of Chapter X.
13. *The Salutation*, i. and iii.
14. Gibbon: *Autobiography.*
15. Wordsworth: *The Excursion.* Preface to Edition of 1814, line 18.
16. Poems of T. Sturge Moore, Collected Edition, Vol. III, p. 57.
17. Ovid: *Metamorphoses*, VII, 20:
    Better things do I see and I esteem them.
18. *The Person.*
19. *Wonder*, I.
20. *The Salutation*, VI.
21. *The Demonstration*, III.
22. *The Salutation*, VII.
23. Tennyson: *Idylls of the King: The Holy Grail.*
24. J. Donne: *Sermons*, p. 135.
25. *Op. cit.*, line 451.
26. John Hall: *A Pastoroll Hymne.*
27. Edmund Spenser: *An Hymne of Heavenly Beautie.*
28. *Nature.*
29. *Speed.*
30. *The Vision.*
31. *The Estate.*
32. Horace: *Odes*, I, i. 36:
    With my exalted head I shall strike the very stars.
33. Berkeley: *Principles of Human Knowledge*, Part I, vi.
34. Boswell's *Johnson*, Chapter XVII.
35. Attributed to R. A. Knox. The second limerick is anonymous.
36. *My Spirit*, III.
37. *Ibid.*, VII.
38. *Thoughts*, I, iv.

39. *Silence.*
40. *My Spirit*, iv.
41. *The Tempest*, IV, i, 153.
42. *Ibid.*, I, ii, 50.
43. *The Improvement*, vi and vii.
44. Wordsworth: *A Poet's Epitaph*, 19.
45. *Op. cit.*, III, 765.
46. *Ibid.*, 783.
47. *The Improvement*, IV.
48. *Op. cit.*, First Century, VIII and X.
49. *Thoughts*, I, 2.
50. Andrew Marvell: *The Garden*.
51. Pensées de Pascal: Article XVIII, xi. Man is but a reed, and that the weakest in nature, but he is *a thinking reed*. The Universe needs not to assume all its armoury to crush him; a vapour, a drop of water, is enough to kill him. But if the Universe were to crush him, man would still be nobler than that by which he is slain, for he *knows* that he dies, but of its power over him the Universe knows nothing.

    All our dignity lies, therefore, in thought. This is the means whereby we must raise ourselves: not by space and time, which we know not how to fill. Therefore *let us strive to think well*; therein lies the moral principle.
52. *Thoughts*, I, v.
53. *Thoughts*, II, iv.
54. *Thoughts*, III.
55. Edward Dyer: *My Mind to Me a Kingdom is.*
56. *The Improvement.*
57. *The Demonstration*, 5–8.
58. *Ibid.*, 4.
59. *Amendment*, 2.
60. W. Macneile Dixon: *Tragedy*, pp. 76–7.
61. *Dumnesse.*
62. *Ibid.*
63. Shelley: *Prometheus Unbound*, II, iv, 72.
64. *Dumnesse.*
65. Wordsworth: *Intimations of Immortality*, 152 ff. See also H. Vaughan, *The Retreate.*
66. *Eden.*
67. *Innocence*, 5. See p. 70.
68. *Blisse.*
69. *Amendment*, 5.
70. *The Recovery.*
71. *Goodnesse*, 1.

72. *The Demonstration*, 8.
73. *The Circulation*, 6.
74. *The Anticipation*, 4.
75. *Ibid.*
76. *Another*, 5.
77. *Thoughts*, IV.
78. *Hymns* [1779], 182. [1933], 375, verse 3.
79. Revelations xxi. 22.
80. *Hymns* [1779], 21, verse 6.
81. *The Approach*, 3.
82. *The Recovery*, 3.
83. *Thanksgiving for the Beauty of His Providence*, p. 237.

Appendix

Berkeley's Theory of Matter, p. 162

I HAVE adopted what might be called the *popular* view of Berkeley's Theory.

Since this volume went to press, there has appeared a very interesting and readable little work by A. A. Luce, Professor of Moral Philosophy in the University of Dublin, entitled *Berkeley's Immaterialism* (Nelson & Son, Ltd.).

Professor Luce maintains that Berkeley was no Subjective Idealist. On the contrary, he expressed his belief in external existence; the reality he denied was that of *Substance*. I take Professor Luce to mean that he regards Berkeley's *Substance* as identical with the *substantia* of the Schoolmen and the ὑποκείμενον of Aristotle, viz. that which was supposed to underlie all sensible phenomena; what Aristotle defined as 'the ultimate substratum which is no longer predicated of anything else' (*Metaphysica*, IV, 8); that is, the residuum when, *in imagination*, all the (*a*) Primary and (*b*) Secondary qualities of Descartes and Locke have been abstracted, viz. such qualities or predicates as (*a*) size, shape, number, motion, and (*b*) colours, tastes, scents and sounds. Berkeley, he maintains, denied the existence of any such residuum, partly on the ground that any sense perception of it would be impossible, for *esse est percipi*; there would be nothing left upon which the sense organs could take hold. Whatever form of existence such an entity might have, it must, in the nature of the case, be non-existent for human intelligence. This interpretation obviously has little, if anything, in common with the thought of Traherne, and incidentally cuts at the very root of the Romish theory of Transubstantiation.

Index

Adam and Eve, 18, 68, 70, 118, 176
Adoration, 50
Æschylus, 85, 148, 149, 172
Affliction, 63
Air, 25
Alcuin, Abbot, 78
Alice through the Looking-glass, 26
Amiel, 11
Anthropomorphism, 178
Apocalyptic, 104
Apocryphal New Testament, 76
Aquinas, Thomas, 45, 81
Aristotle, 134, 136, 194
Assurance, Christian, 29
Astronomy, 111
Atheism, 93
Atonement, 45 ff., 49, 180
Attributes, Divine, 167
Augustus Cæsar, 51, 52
Authority in Religion, 128, 131

Bacchæ, The, 140, 141
Bacon, Francis, 69, 136, 138
Bacon, Roger, 84
Barth, Karl, 182
Baxter, Richard, 125
Beaumont and Fletcher, 80
Behmen, 15, 184
Berdyaev, Nicolas, 88, 154
Berkeley, Bishop, 161 ff., 194
Bevan, Edwyn, 9
Bibliolatry, 133
Birds, 25, 113
Birth, 155
Blake, William, 108

Blood of Christ, 45
Body, The, 78, 81, 119, 120, 155, 156
Botticelli, 31
Bowls, 23
Bridges, Robert, xii, 65, 166, 167
Brooke, Rupert, 86
Browne, Sir Thomas, 67, 103, 153
Bunyan, John, 31, 100, 109, 121, 145, 181
Burnet, Bishop, 102
Burns, Robert, 53
Butler, Samuel, 109
Byron, Lord, 108

Calvinism, 141
Cambridge Platonists, 100 ff.
Canticles (Song of Solomon), 29
Carlyle, Thomas, 85, 116
Carroll, Lewis, 26
Charles I, King, 16
Chaucer, Geoffrey, 3, 113
Chesterton, G. K., 22
Children, 31, 70, 157, 173 ff.
Church, The, 58
  English, 3
  infallible, 131
Civil War, The, 35
Clement of Alexandria, 100
Coercion, 127, 139
Coleridge, S. T., 9, 55, 104, 144
Conceit, 122
Conscience, 142
Consistency, 24
Contradiction, Law of, 134
Contrition, 29
Conversation, 121

Copernicus, 14, 68, 69
Cosmic Harmony, 69
Cosmology, 68
Cowley, Abraham, 35
Cowper, William, 6, 125
Crabbe, George, 121, 150
Crashaw, Richard, x, 34 ff., 95, 173, 186
Creation, 88
  of souls, 87
Cross, The, 6, 34, 37, 43, 44, 180
Crucifix, 34, 38, 44
Crucifixion, The, 38, 40, 44, 46
Cruelty, 42
Cynicism, 100
Cyrus, 62

DANCING, 69
Daniel, Book of, 104
Dante, 31, 45, 119
Darwin, Charles, 154
Davies, Sir John, x, 60 ff., 187
Dawn, 110
Death, 13, 92, 96
  of Christ, 46
Deism, 146
Deities, classical, 18
de la Mare, Walter, 41, 86, 162
Delphi, 64, 75
Descartes, 70, 138
Desire, 179
Despair, 86
De Stogumber, 42
Devil, 19
Dilemma, 135
Dion of Syracuse, 107
Divus Augustus, 52
Dixon, W. Macneile, 172
Dobell, Bertram, 150
Donne, John, 2, 27, 40, 98, 119, 120, 125, 158
Dryden, John, 36, 121
Dyer, Edward, 170

EARLE, JOHN, 70
Earth, The, 25
Ecclesiasticism, 113
Ecstasy, 139
Eden, 18, 27
Elizabeth, Queen, 98
Elizabethan Age, 69, 75
Elizabethan poetry, 1, 23
Elizabethan psychology, 79
Emanation, 88
Emblems, 16
Emerson, R.W., 24, 100, 112
Enoch, 182
Enthusiasm, 139
Environment, 157, 164
Epicureanism, 88
Error, 74
Eternal *Now*, 178
Euripides, 32, 131
Euthydemus, 75
Eve, 18, 120
Evil, 20, 72, 73
Experience, 30

Faerie Queene, The, 112
Failure, 59
Fall of Man, the, 18, 68
Falstaff, 24
Faust, 6
Felicity, 150 ff.
Fish, 26
Fletcher, Phineas, 39
Food, 25
Forgiveness, 7
France, Anatole, 113
Francis of Assisi, 26
Freedom, religious, 127

GAMES, 23
Generation, 88
Gibbon, Edward, 155
Gilbert, W. S., 101
God, 110, 119

God, seeing, 66
   and Man, 172, 176
   doctrine of, 177
Golden Age, 20, 21
Grace of God, 9
Grantly, Archdeacon, 129
Greek thought, 172

HALL, JOHN, 158
Hamlet, 117
Happiness, 179
   of God, 170
Hastings, Lady Margaret, 62
Hayward, Sir John, 113
Heaven, 14, 55
Helen of Troy, 85 ff.
Hell, 42
Henrietta Maria, Queen, 35
Henry V, King, 106
Herbert, George, 1, 180
Hereafter, the, 13, 112
Hobbes, Thomas, 70, 101, 138
Holy Spirit, the, 135
Honour, 24
Horace, 160
Hudibras, 109
Humour, 122, 184
Huntingdon, Selina, Countess of, 62
Huxley, Julian, 105
Hymn-book, Methodist, 7, 15, 32, 45 ff., 147, 148

IDIOCY, 94
Ignorance, 74
Immaterial, The, 164
Immortality, 14, 60, 77, 82, 91, 112
Imponderables, the, 167
Incarnation, the, 36, 52
Inconsistency, 24
Infallibility, 131
Infancy, 173, 175
Inge, R.W., 143

Ingham, Benjamin, 62
Innocence, 71, 176
Ireland, 61

JACQUES, 115
James I, King, 61
James, M. R., 76
Jesus Christ, 26, 36, 50, 76, 158
Joan of Arc, 41 ff.
Johnson, Dr. Samuel, 162
Jove, 21, 87
Jowett, Benjamin, 100
Joy, 30, 156, 171, 181
Julian of Norwich, 67
Julius Cæsar, 38, 41
Juvenal, 37, 64

KEATS, JOHN, 53
Kierkegaard, 119
Kingdom of God, 58, 76
Kingswood School, 23
Knowledge, desire for, 71

La Giaconda, 85
Latitudinarians, 102
Laughter, 115
Law, 77
Law, William, 15
Lightfoot, Bishop, 48
Logia of Oxyrhynchus, 76
Logic, 136, 148
Lucretius, 88, 137

MAN, 28, 49, 64
   and God, 119, 172, 176
   and the World, 164
Marcus Aurelius, 82
Mark Antony, 38
Marlowe, Chris., 6, 85
Martin, Richard, 60, 61
Martyrdom, 54
Marvell, Andrew, 168
Mary Magdalene, 36

Masefield, John, 43
Medea, The, 32
Memory, 83
Menelaus, 86
Meonic, 88, 89, 154
Metaphysics, 148
Methodist Revival, 147
Midnight, 11
Milton, John, 15, 18, 20, 27, 33, 50, 58, 67, 68, 71, 73, 103, 118, 120
Mimicry, 117
Mind, 166, 170
Minerva, 87
More, Henry, x, 100 ff., 189
Murray, Sir Gilbert, 32, 85, 141, 148
Mysticism, 15 ff., 29
Mythology, classical, 18

NAMES, 105
Narcissus, 119
Nashe, Thomas, 27, 86
Nativity, the, 51, 52
Nature, 9 f., 25, 159, 160, 171
New Jerusalem, the, 181
Newton, Sir Isaac, 15
Nicodemus, 12
Night, 12, 111
Noah, 94
Nonsense, 115 f.

OBJECTIVE WORLD, THE, 94, 157
Old age, 94
Omar Khayyám, ix
Origen, 100
Original sin, 90
Orphism, 82, 90
Ovid, 119
Oxford, 10, 60, 61, 62

PAGANISM, 18

Pantheism, 177
Paradise, 27, 68
Parrot, 115
Parsons, 124 f.
Particulars, 84
Pascal, Blaise, 132, 168, 193
Pater, Walter, 85
Paul, St., 7, 25, 48, 73, 157
Peace, 33
Pelican, 45
Perception, sense, 137
Perfection, 71
Philosophy, 104, 144
Piety, 117
Pilgrim's Progress, The, 100, 109, 121, 145, 181
Pistol, 106
Plato, 81, 84, 90, 100, 104, 107, 109
Pliable, 109
Plotinus, 104, 109
Plutarch, 107
Poetry, 144
Polonius, 117
Pope, Alexander, 17, 36, 137, 150
Popularity, 106 f.
Possession, 157
Power, 130
Praise, 50
Prayer, 8 f.
Preaching, 125
Pre-natal existence, 153
Prior, Matthew, 72, 74
Prometheus, 172
Prospero, 69
Psalms, the, 10, 12, 28, 91, 138
Ptolemy, 68, 73
Punishment, future, 93
Puritanism, 23, 140

QUARLES, FRANCIS, x, 15 ff.; 59, 73, 184
Quiller-Couch, Sir Arthur, 49, 181

REASON, 74, 95, 132, 136
Reconciliation, 29
Redemption, 37, 42, 78
Religion, 58, 95, 147
Repentance, 8, 29
Revelation, 158
Ritualism, 123, 126
Roman Catholicism, 37
Romeo and Juliet, 105

Saint Joan, 42, 116
St. John, 45, 177
St. John of the Cross, 21
Saints, 12
Salvation, 4, 42, 43
Santa Teresa, 53 ff.
Sartor Resartus, 116
Satan, 72
Satire, 122, 146
Saturn, 21
Scholasticism, 129, 134, 178
Science, 161, 167
Scripture, 133
Sea, 25
Sectaries, 100, 101, 114, 145, 190
Seeking God, 29
Self, the, 63, 152
Self-knowledge, 65, 75
Self-love, 119
Self-possession, 59
Sense, 138
Seraph, 57
Sermons, 125
Serpent, the, 18
Seventeenth century, the, x, 20
Shakespeare, 21, 24, 26, 31, 38, 62, 85, 105, 106, 115, 117, 150, 166
Shaw, George Bernard, 42, 116
Shelley, P. B., 101, 175
Shepherds, 51, 52
Sin, 5, 6, 21, 48, 49, 173
Singing, 37, 39

Snobbery, 107
Socrates, 64, 65, 75, 80, 84
Sorley, W. R., 102
Soul, the, 60, 67, 77, 78, 81, 87, 91, 94
Southey, Robt., 144, 145
Space, 83, 165
Spain, 57
Speech, 173, 174, 175
Spenser, Edmund, 104, 112, 159
Spinoza, 179
Spirit, of God, 135
Squeers, Fanny, 65
Stars, 10 ff.
Stevenson, R. L., 152
Sturge Moore, Thos., 155
Style, ix
Subjective idealism, 161 ff., 194
Sublimation, 84
Suffering, 42
Supercilious, 101
Swift, Jonathan, 122, 132
Swinburne, 36, 150

TALKATIVE, MR., 121
Taylor, Jeremy, 80, 83, 125
Tears, 37, 39
Teleology, 160
Tempest, The, 166
Temptation, 72
Ten Commandments, the, 25
Tennyson, Alfred, 4, 19, 63, 158
Testament of Beauty, The, xii, 65, 166, 167
Theism, 177
Thompson, Francis, 9, 38
Thought, 164, 167 ff.
Tibullus, 21
Tillyard, E. M. W., 68
Time, 87, 165, 168
Timidity, religious, 24
Tobacco, 24
Touchstone, 116

Traherne, Thomas, xi, 150 ff., 191
Trinity, doctrine of the, 110
Trollope, Anthony, 129

UNIFORMITY, 126
Universals, 84
Universe, the, 110, 160

VALUES, 170
Vaughan, Henry, x, 1 ff., 83, 150, 183
Venus, 22
Virgil, 20, 32, 51
Virgin Mary, the, 40, 44, 49

WALLER, EDMUND, 82
Walton, Izaak, 3
Watson, William, 96
Watts, G. F., 22
Watts, Isaac, 50, 182
Wesley, Charles, xii, 7, 21, 30, 44 ff., 95, 153, 181

Wesley, John, xii, 15, 23, 62, 64, 80, 89, 97, 98, 106, 147, 148, 180, 184
Whichcote, Benjamin, 80, 102
Whitehead, A. N., 146
Whitman, Walt, 66, 77
Whyte, Alexander, 54
Willey, Basil, 103
Wilson, J. Dover, 73
Wonders, 156
Wordsworth, William, 58, 67, 151, 155, 166, 175
World, the, 22, 58, 164
Wotton, Sir Henry, 10
Wounds of Jesus, 38

XENOPHON, 62, 75

YOUTH, 142

ZEUS, 172

www.ingramcontent.com/pod-product-compliance
Lightning Source LLC
Chambersburg PA
CBHW060606230426
43670CB00011B/2000